5

THOUGHTS ON CONDUCTING

Sir Adrian Boult.

ADRIAN C. BOULT 1889-

Thoughts on Conducting

Phoenix House Ltd

London

CONTENTS

❧ v ❧

To
A. M. G. B.

ILLUSTRATIONS

ACKNOWLEDGMENT

I must place on record my indebtedness to three people without whose help this book could never have been finished: Mrs Gwendolen Beckett, Mr Peter Gellhorn, Mr Scott Goddard.

Foreword

THERE have appeared in the last few years several fine
books by experienced conductors which are full of ripe
wisdom and invaluable hints for young conductors, so it
may well be asked what need there is for another book on
the subject. The excuse must be based on the fact that the
art of conducting is so much newer than any other form
of musical technique that it is only now in process of
forming itself into various schools, such as we know so
well in singing, string-playing, and the pianoforte.

This book is an attempt to define the necessary elements
in acquiring a workable conducting technique, and to
place on record the methods of various conductors of
note. Among these some prominence will be given to
Arthur Nikisch who, jointly occupying the desks of the
Leipzig Gewandhaus and Berlin Philharmonic Orchestras before and during the 1914 war, made a very deep
impression wherever he went, and, while commanding
an extraordinarily warm personal tone-colour in any
orchestra he handled, and arousing much excitement over
his 'mesmeric' qualities, was at the same time, albeit
unconsciously, the master of what now seems an in-
credibly economical, powerful, and expressive technique
of the stick, a description of which is our main purpose
here.

Nikisch was a picturesque figure. Unusually small of
stature, he used to tell a story of hearing a lady say to her

friend: 'Look, there's a pocket Nikisch', as he walked into a restaurant. He was very proud of his tiny white hands and had them half covered by an enormous shirt cuff which made them look even smaller. He always moved very slowly, and at concerts he had a unique habit of resisting the temptation that assails most of us, of rushing for the artists' room the moment the music is over. He would acknowledge the applause for some time, then perhaps turn and chat with some of the orchestra; then come forward again and bow. This might happen several times before he would feel that the *diminuendo* of applause enabled him to make a slow, uninterrupted exit.

His economy of gesture was extraordinary. I remember one night at the Gewandhaus we had had a rather too exciting performance of a Brahms symphony (at least to my solidly Richter-guided upbringing). I suddenly realized that Nikisch's hand had never been raised above the level of his face; one felt that a stretch to arm's length would have caused an earthquake. At the same time, as a musician, he could not command universal approval. I have just listened to his recording of the Fifth Beethoven, and was greatly astonished at the little *accelerandos* and *rallentandos* which have been freely brought into the first and last movements. These would have shocked Dr Hans Richter deeply; indeed they did, as I heard from a friend of his at the time. And I remember that even in my wildest youthful excitement I used to say that if I were asked to write a list of the music I would prefer to hear conducted by Nikisch than by anyone else, I could only make a short list. The mercurial Wagner of *Tristan* would be his, but the measured and solid *Meistersinger* was the property of Hans Richter, who seemed as the last act went forward to identify himself with the lovable and similar figure of Hans Sachs on the stage, and the tributes of the people of Nuremberg seemed matched by the affection of his players for the great conductor.

The love for Richter, shown again and again by the orchestras of London and Manchester, was originally begotten of fear. It was in the 1880's that he first came to London. A grumpy German, muttering in his beard, with a piercing eye that missed little, there seemed nothing about him that could endear him to anyone, and orchestras (a good deal tougher in those days) disliked him more and more. One day at rehearsal he presumed to tell a horn player in some detail how to play a certain passage. 'It can't be done that way, doctor', was the risky reply. 'Ah, so, indeed; please pass me your instrument.' Richter then played the passage, to the great discomfiture of the owner of the horn, and indeed of the whole orchestra, who all now wondered if he could play *their* instruments as well as the horn, and weren't going to take the risk of putting it to the test. He thus became a legend of omniscience.

He told a mutual friend that when he lived with Wagner he undertook to make a copy of the full score of *Die Meistersinger* as Wagner wrote out the orchestration. They worked in different rooms, and the sheets were taken to Richter as Wagner finished them. He said it always took him an hour or so longer each day to do the copying than Wagner took over the scoring. As anyone who has studied the published facsimile of that full score will remember, Wagner's neat hand bears no trace of haste, and there are few corrections. The act of orchestration was itself faster than the act of copying.

Richter then, to me in my youth, was the supreme interpreter of Beethoven, of Brahms (though, later, Steinbach's eloquent readings seemed more convincing), and of the more static Wagner. He had taken part in the first performance of the *Siegfried Idyll*, and I always noticed that he used all the strings he could get hold of. Not for him the seventeen-player stunts, which no doubt have their time and place on certain occasions, and throw into relief the solo woodwind parts in one or two of the *tuttis*.

Now for the Nikisch list. I have said that *Tristan* was his, and only his at that time. Indeed, I can conceive nothing more electric and memorable than two performances I heard him give in one week in Covent Garden in the winter of 1906. He also directed the *Dutchman* and *Freischütz* in that week—a revelation for a seventeen-year-old. Other performances I can remember with special excitement are the Liszt rhapsodies and tone poems, the Weber overtures, Schumann, and, curiously, the Verdi *Requiem*, in which he had played in Vienna as a student under the composer's direction. Many people would have said Tchaikovsky, but for me Safonoff's performances were far more powerful and manly and less neurotic. But to Nikisch must go the credit for the revival of Tchaikovsky's Fifth, which the composer himself thought was a failure.

I hope that this book, though written largely for the general reader, may also be of some use to the student conductor, in so far as it attempts to describe the methods and achievements of several outstanding conductors, seen through the eyes of one enthusiastic student.

It is an unfortunate thing that the conductor's job, even when we over-exert ourselves as most of us do, looks quite easy and, what is more, glamorous, for, like playing the organ, it gives a great sense of power.

I still get many letters from young people who are (usually for no reason at all) convinced that they are potentially heaven-sent conductors. In my B.B.C. days they pleaded for ten minutes or longer of the rehearsal time of the B.B.C. Symphony Orchestra, after which, they were convinced, they would at once be flooded with engagements. This pathetic state of mind is so common that I have prepared a formidable list of qualifications for the practising conductor. Here they are:

1. He should be a master of four or five orchestral instruments.

2. He should have played in an orchestra for some years, perhaps on different instruments.

3. He should have had similar experience in a choral society.

4. He should have a very full knowledge of the whole classical repertoire from the point of view of orchestration, structure, phrasing, etc.

5. He should have a clear pattern in his mind of the necessities of style in performance in regard to the many different schools of music which the normal conductor must tackle.

6. He must have a power of leadership, an infinite capacity for taking pains, unlimited patience, and a real gift of psychology. He must have a constitution of iron and be ready to appear good-humoured in face of the most maddening frustrations.

7. He must be a master of the actual control of the stick. This may look easy but needs a good deal of thought and hard practice.

8. He must also have knowledge of musical history and of all great music: songs, organ, chamber music, pianoforte, etc.

9. He should be a connoisseur of many other forms of art.

I may add that there are a number of young men whose qualifications include all, or nearly all, of the above, but who are unable to find conducting jobs in this country. It would therefore be unwise for any musician to do anything to add to their number. I consider that on a number of occasions I have done really good work when I have persuaded people who have come to see me to take up some business opportunity and keep music for their spare time. Some of them have written to me at a later date and said what a happy time they are having in operatic, choral, or orchestral societies in their evenings, while their days are spent in other work which is not too uncongenial.

In other words, music is an excellent servant but not too good a mistress.

I have also known people, who are working in some big firm, who have been able to collect a number of their business colleagues and form excellent orchestras, choirs, or brass bands.

I admit that it would not be true to say that every well-known conductor has this complete list at his finger tips, but most of them are absolutely essential, and perhaps the most important of all—a power of command over others and (still more vital) over oneself—is hardest to explain to many candidates who quite clearly don't possess it. I remember in my Royal College of Music days a student made a rather stupid mistake and I afterwards asked him why he did it. I knew he was much too good a musician to have done such a thing in the normal way. 'Well, you see, I find that the minute I get a bit of wood in my hand it seems to deprive me automatically of the use of nine-tenths of my brain.' It is quite impossible to imagine the paralysis that can come when first standing up to the ordeal of the direction of a rehearsal. My own initiation was most fortunately gradual and progressive. I was able to begin in quite a small way, and gradually work my way to things of greater importance, but it was for a long time a sort of nightmare obsession with me, that if I suddenly had the chance to stand before a really first-class body of players, I might play through the first piece and their performance would be so perfect that I could find nothing at all to say and I should have to retire ignominiously. When I hear the things that young conductors say to experienced players I sometimes wish that my nightmare could be applied to them.

I think I should tell of a physical experience that came to me when I started working with the brand-new B.B.C. Symphony Orchestra at the age of forty-one. The dynamic and cultural range at the disposal of these splendid players was so much greater than anything I had experienced before that I soon found myself stiffening seriously at both ends of the scale: *ppp* and *fff*. My shoulders and the back of my neck hardened so much and so often that I had to go every few weeks to an osteopath to get myself broken apart and fixed. I did all I could to learn to relax, but it seemed impossible to communicate the tension I wanted without tensing myself, and I knew that if I persisted I was heading for the neuritis and arthritis from which many conductors do in fact suffer. Finally, I found great help from the Mensendieck method, still practised in London by Mrs Harriet Nyemann, who provided exercises to strengthen certain muscles in shoulder and back, so that this strain and tension could be suggested and communicated without actually suffering myself.

December 1962.   A. B.

1

Technique

ALL musical performance, whatever the size of the forces involved, must be controlled by one person. In chamber music the first violin is usually also the leader and director of rehearsals, but an *ensemble* of more than eight players or singers is usually directed by a conductor who is himself silent and uses a white stick in order to make his directions clear. It is desirable, though not often practicable, that the players and singers should know their part by heart in order that they can give the conductor their undivided attention. But this involves intense and prolonged preparation, so a system is usually practised by which they learn to read their music almost continuously, while at the same time they can see the movements of the conductor's stick just over the top of their music, and it is wise for the conductor to restrict his movements to a field which will keep them all well inside this secondary vision of the performer. In other words, if the conductor's gestures are sometimes high over his head and at others down by his knees, he will be difficult to follow, and in the same way if the performer is sitting or standing in such a way that he can only see the conductor out of the corner of his eye, he will not be able to immerse himself so well in the *ensemble*.

Almost all the great conductors of the past stood absolutely still. Richter usually stood on a small stand not much larger than an ordinary shoe box. The picturesque habit of walking about and miming the music like a ballet dancer is a modern development, which I dare say will appeal to some of the less sophisticated members of our audience. But it doesn't make matters easier for the players and singers, and I am inclined to think that it is only when he has complete control of himself that a con-ductor can hope to control other people. Like a good singer, the conductor should, I think, rest most of his weight well forward on his feet; if he can lift his heels without effort the balance should be good, but if his toes can easily be raised, the weight will be thrown too far back, and the power from his stick will be apt to go over people's heads.

In thinking of the amazing economy of Nikisch's stick I can remember two striking things that were said about him at the time of his death. Someone suggested that if he were put into a glass box and told to conduct something, one could recognize the work he had chosen before he had done more than ten bars. I wonder if this was the exaggeration it now sounds. I would give a good deal to possess a short film of Nikisch in action. Tovey once said: 'If Bach's works were all lost and only a perfectly correct account of them remained, that account would not be believed for a moment.' It is hard now to believe that Nikisch could do all he seemed to be doing at that time, but the fact remains that his rehearsals were over in no time, and he spoke comparatively little with his voice, because the eloquence of his stick by itself produced nearly all the results he wanted.

The other impressive point which I saw in one of the obituaries and could confirm from my own observation was that his left hand had never been seen to copy what his right hand was doing, except perhaps for one bar at a climax, never more. Mr Walter Legge recently coined the expression 'Grecian urn action' for the ugly modern habit of conducting with both elbows at once, and keeping left and right arms pumping in exactly the same way.

I feel that the cause of a great deal of this awkward-looking action is that it *feels* much more powerful and more impressive to work with both hands at once. Unfortunately it doesn't *look* so; what we *feel* like and what we *look* like are two very different things, and conductors who cannot trust themselves to keep control on this are earnestly recommended to find a critical friend who will keep an eye on them. A good deal can be done by watching one's action in a distant looking-glass, but a human critic is better, and I can strongly recommend from my own experience a firmly critical wife who will constantly watch for any lapse in deportment.

The point of the stick, then, is the focus of the whole contact between conductor and orchestra, and if the stick is held firmly, as can be seen so often, with a stiff wrist and the pivotal joint back at the elbow, it follows that there can be little or no expressive life in the point of the stick; the stick and arm form one inflexible rod, and there is nothing but the elbow to direct the performance as to *ensemble*, pace, and expression.

With Nikisch, fingers, wrists, and elbow were supple

and free. He held the stick with two fingers and thumb, the two fingers separated by about a finger's width, the thumb exactly opposite this space, so that there was a powerful leverage. One can easily get this feeling with a pencil held at right angles to the fingers, and then if the stick is slightly turned over so that it forms, as it were, an elongation of the thumb, an easy flexible grip can be achieved. A wide circle can then be described by the point of the stick, and only when something wider is needed should the wrist, and finally the elbow, join in the proceedings. Often when the fingers were giving, say, a *mezzo forte* four in a bar, the wrist would just come in to carry the beat over the bar line. Albert Coates—a distinguished Nikisch pupil—used to talk of 'Etagen'; each beat was a little higher than the last up to the end of the bar, with a final lift before the down beat.

I have said that Nikisch's hands were very small and his fingers thin. It was easy for him to hold a thin wooden stick, but I am afraid that many of us have larger hands and damper fingers, and it is essential that the grip should never stiffen, as it must if the fingers become damp. In this case I recommend, and use myself, a number of rubber bands round the handle, which make it easy to hold the stick quite loosely without fear of dropping it.

The balance of the stick is important, and I find the so-called Porteous baton, marketed by Messrs Chester of Great Marlborough Street, W.1, to be the most comfortable I have ever held. Colonel Porteous was a distinguished irrigation engineer who came to see me soon after I went to the B.B.C. He said he had attended a conductors' class with me years before and had then asked a lot of questions, pondering which he evolved the stick, slightly weighted at the handle end, which gives one a fine sense of control and expression. I remember Joseph Lewis coming into my room when Colonel Porteous was with me. He picked up one of the sticks, and said: 'This is the best I have ever used.' I had just made the same remark.

If anyone suggests the use of the hand for conducting I always reply that only when one has achieved this finger freedom and consequently eloquent use of the stick can one possibly claim to know when to use a stick and when not. Anyone who stands four or five yards from a looking-glass and compares the effect of his bare hand with that of a white enamel stick cannot fail to agree that the hand needs a great deal more looking at to get its message.

What, then, are the principles behind our manipulation of the point of our stick, once we have gained control of it? I think any observant concert-goer will remember having seen a bright, jerky little beat trying to coax a *largo cantabile* from some patient choir or orchestra, and this obvious contrast between what the stick looks like and the sound that should be expected (and is indeed often achieved in spite of the inappropriate gestures of the conductor) shows at any rate what not to do.

It is not easy to describe how the movements of a stick can be made expressive. A jumpy beat—one that springs up immediately the beat has occurred—is obviously the essence of *staccato*. *Legato* is harder to suggest and harder to do; in fact plenty of well-known conductors can make people play and sing *legato* without showing it at all in their sticks, but I cannot believe that their authority would not be greater, and their achievement at rehearsal quicker and more effective, if they took the trouble to make their sticks move in a more expressive way.

Imagine, for instance, a stick which drops, say, on to a table, and the point then strokes the table and gradually forms the partial loop which should always show the stick's progress to the next beat, and the kind of expression which fills the space between each beat. This outline of the basis of expression in the work of the stick can be extended to cover many points of expression—*crescendo, diminuendo, sforzando,* and many others.

In examining the space between beats it is perhaps as well to begin with the simplest pattern of a start. I suggest that the stick should be brought to the most convenient position for gathering attention; it will naturally rest there until audience and performers are ready; then the point will slowly rise and, proceeding gradually faster, will form a loop finishing exactly at the point from which it started. The pace at which the point moves accelerates steadily, and it comes back to the point of rest quickly, stopping with something of a jerk, and passing immediately through this to the next beat by means of a similar loop. The stick should never stop unless the rhythm of the music is broken, and between each beat there should be this steady increase of pace, so that players can feel just where they are between beats, as well as seeing the beat itself.

The left hand should be kept for any expression which is, so to speak, beyond the vocabulary of an expressive stick. It must not just duplicate the work of the stick.

2

Preparation

THE problem of how to absorb quickly and permanently the new music that comes one's way for performance may well be solved in many different ways by different interpreters. I don't know: I have rarely discussed it with colleagues, and I have seen little about it in books.

Perhaps we should begin a description of the process by a moment's thought on the ultimate aim of musical performance. I feel very strongly that the aspect which must be uppermost in mind must be the inevitability of the music in its passage from start to finish. When it has been apprehended as one eloquent whole, in architectural terms as 'a splendid elevation', its power, its beauty, its many other qualities take their places in this total structure, and in due proportion.

Now I find that this total picture is best taken in if the score is first read through somewhat faster than its appropriate performing pace. I go through it several times in this rapid way—naturally not hearing it as a complete score, but noting its shape, its balance, the structure of its keys, its climaxes, emotional and dynamic;

and getting, as it were, a bird's-eye view. Then, particularly if it is a complex modern work, will come the examination of detail, perhaps taking difficult passages to the pianoforte, but relating them continually to the main lines of the work as one goes along. I think it is wise to get to know the music very well indeed before one begins to think about the actual interpretation of it. It is surely dangerously easy to begin thinking of effective *rubatos*, extra *crescendos*, and so on, when one is in a state of half-knowledge, which will only lead to extravagances and 'new readings' which may tickle the minority but cannot impress the saner part of our audience as a sound and vital performance. I would rather risk giving a performance which reflected so accurately the printed page that some people might call it dull than embellish my reading with so many frills and extras that the main message of the work was in danger of getting concealed.

There is an aspect of this thorough knowledge which I have experienced on many occasions, and can only hope it shows a result of the right kind of absorption. Going out for a walk by myself I would start thinking through some work that I had in preparation. As I went on I might be interrupted; someone might ask me the way, or some longer incident might break into my internal concert, and it might go out of my mind for several minutes. At the end of this I would resume my walk, and find that the performance had gone on unconsciously, and I might even find that I had got into the next movement. At first I thought this was all wrong, but later I felt that it must show that the work was firmly in my mind, and the subconscious had taken it over for a time, as it equally might have to do if there were some interruption at a concert which could not be allowed to break into the performance.

PREPARATION

Having thoroughly soaked in the work, how are we going to face the problem of turning it into sound? The basic style must now come uppermost, and valuable books have been published by experts in the very many fields into which our work will take us. I do not think this is the place to lay down the law on the matter of style in performance; in Palestrina are we thinking of pure, cool sound or are we going to let the dramatic side of it come uppermost? If it is Johann Sebastian Bach, how much are we going to add to the very sparse expression marks? How are we going to fill in the *continuo* part—on organ, harpsichord, or pianoforte? In this connection it doesn't seem to be remembered that Willem Mengelberg in his annual *St Matthew Passion* performance in Amsterdam used in the recitatives an identical harpsichord and organ part so that the impact of each chord sounded like the harpsichord, but the organ could sustain where the harpsichord couldn't. In Haydn and Mozart, how much are we going to add to those composers who only later in life heard an orchestral *crescendo*? Or are we just going to play what is there with beautiful tone and feeling? So with Beethoven: are the shortcomings of his scoring to be bolstered up, whether they come from the incomplete scale of the brass instruments, or from the altered weight and power of modern instruments, or from the miscalculations of his deafness?

When we come to more modern things the problems alter somewhat; in romantic music we can allow ourselves some freedom of pace, for instance. In Beethoven symphonies I can usually find a *tempo* which will sound right for the whole movement, but I allow myself some freedom in the overtures, and I find the first movement of the Schubert C major needs a slightly slower pace for

the second subject, if we can achieve it surreptitiously!
I wonder that people don't think a little more about the
nature of the composer whose problems they are solving.
I get most annoyed, for instance, when I hear people
tidying up the tune in the *poco sostenuto* of the *Scherzo* of
the 'New World' Symphony. When the clarinets take
over this tune from the flute and oboe they alter one note
in the second bar. Why shouldn't they? Who knows that
Dvořák wanted it to be played exactly the same every
time? Of course every German conductor *must* tidy it up,
but I really cannot see why. It isn't Mozart!

Brahms is another matter; many of his movements can
go through at a uniform speed, but some want shaping, I
think. I feel very strongly about minuets and trios.
Surely they are one dance which is danced straight
through, and doesn't want a little gap after the minuet or
anywhere else, or for the matter of that a *rallentando* at the
end. A minuet like that in the Mozart G minor sounds
quite enchanting when it plays itself out in strict time—
as if someone had shut a door and it was still going on
behind it.

There is a story that Toscanini was raging round the
artists' room at Carnegie Hall in the interval of a concert
in his usual agony of nerves. A friend tried to comfort
him: 'Maestro, why are you nervous now? You only have
the C minor to do and that went magnificently in Brooklyn last night.'

'Brooklyn last night?' was the agonized reply. 'But the
tempi last night were ALL WRONG. I must get them better
tonight.'

I like to think of that story whenever I am tempted to
think I have done a fairly good job.

This matter of fundamental pace is the conductor's

gravest problem, and I do not think one can ever feel that it is finally solved anywhere. It depends on so many circumstances—hall, players, weather, audience, and the eternal question: Do I really know this work?

In faster movements the problem becomes easier, because it is more dependent on practical considerations: the skill of the players, the properties of the hall, and so on. Slower movements become more and more difficult. With Beethoven in particular the first bars of slow movements often look deceptively slow, and I always believe in thinking of a passage later in the movement (perhaps somewhere where there are a large number of notes to the bar) before starting. It is, I think, possible to find a pace, even in the slow movements of the third and seventh Symphonies, which can be held throughout the movement, though most people allow themselves to speed up a little in the fugal passages.

Haydn's *andantes* in 2–4 also seem to me often played too slowly; they should surely move in a gentle crotchet lilt and not a ponderous quaver *adagio*. With Bach, too, widely different *tempi* seem to be chosen by performers who can all command our respect.

It is not generally known that most watches and small clocks tick 300 to the minute; accordingly the metronome speeds of 150 (two ticks), 100 (three ticks), 75, 60, 50 can easily be found on any watch, and this will enable one to dispense with the noisy horrors that some people use.

There are a number of other considerations connected with the preparation of scores which may perhaps be thought about here. I often wonder whether absolute pitch is the blessing that some people think it to be. It is of course a help when unravelling a complicated modern score. One can spot a wrong accidental simply by know-ing it is wrong. On the other hand a keen relative sense of pitch is far more scholarly, and I for one confess that I would prefer it if I had the choice. Contrary to general belief absolute pitch can be taught, and the late Edward Maryon, some of whose operas had a considerable vogue in Germany some fifty years ago, had a successful method of linking pitch with colour. Sir Percy Buck used to say that his father took him to the piano when he was about seven and hammered on one note saying: 'Now, that is G, and don't you forget it.' He said that he never did!

How much should one write in a score? Personally I feel that if possible nothing should be written at all. Sir John Barbirolli has said that he prefers to spend the time learning the music rather than scribbling in it; and I feel that the only justification for these signposts in the score is when one expects to be very tired, as, for instance, in a long series of nightly concerts. It is, I believe, difficult to learn to walk without crutches if you have once used them, and the same applies here. There is also a consider-able danger that if the scores are heavily marked, they will tend to congeal your performance; it will always be exactly the same. You will think only of the marks and forget the music. My colleague M. Inghelbrecht has a most amusing chapter in his book on conducting on what he calls *graffiti* which conductors scrawl all over hired scores.

It is another matter when we talk about marking the players' parts. Here, in particular, bowings for the strings, also breathing marks for long wind passages, are most important. Uniform bowing is agreed to be the right practice for string playing nowadays. It was rarely seen in England in my young days, but players do everything possible to achieve it now. The leader, or sometimes the conductor, marks the parts beforehand, and may make slight modifications at the first rehearsal. Extra expression marks can sometimes be added, and a good librarian may spot a place where the copyist or engraver has come to the end of his page at a point where it is all wrong for half the players to stop playing for a moment while they turn. A bar or two can be written in the margin to put this right.

I would like to return to the difficulty of knowing whether one really has learned a score through and through, and so really is in a position to take a rehearsal and presume to dictate to men many of whom may well be twice as experienced and knowledgeable as is their conductor.

I recommend concentration on one edition of any work to be studied. I believe actors find it confusing to study a part from different editions, and I certainly find myself badly put out if I ever have to use a different edition from that to which I am accustomed; so I still use miniature scores in some cases.

Admittedly most of these are of familiar works which I do know by heart. I need the score at rehearsal in order to have the section letters available, but I don't use the score much at performances though I always have it at hand.

I can sympathize with the young conductor who wants absolutely nothing between him and the orchestra, and nothing within reach that he can possibly hit with his stick. When he gets older he will probably come to like the feel of the desk in front of him (perhaps a little to his left), on which he can put his stick instead of having to walk about with it before and after the music. There is no doubt that there is an extra freedom in control when one is absolutely independent of the score and the music unfolds in the mind so that the eyes are devoted to our colleagues on the platform and never need look down to the score, but there are moments in modern works when most of us have to refer to memory in a conscious way; this must be some distraction in the process of pouring the music as we feel it out to the performers, and it is for each one of us to decide whether a glance at the score is going to interrupt that flow less than a conscious effort of memory.

It is interesting that many more concerto players are now using their music at performances, even though they hardly look at it. I believe that some American conductors have been forced to include in their contracts a clause promising never to use a score at concerts. It is incredible that any member of a governing body of an orchestra could be so stupid as to agree to a clause which must inevitably restrict the repertoire of an orchestra. I can remember being most impressed in the great days of Stokowski at Philadelphia by seeing a liveried attendant suddenly appear with a desk and a score. A new work of Stravinsky's was on the programme, and the great man had no doubt a good reason for having the score at hand, though his memory is known to be phenomenal.

3

Rehearsal

I IMAGINE that an enterprising journalist (and his
readers) could have an amusing time if he could
persuade a few orchestral players to describe in detail
the rehearsal methods of the conductors they know!
Perhaps the names should be withheld—in fact, an
intriguing guessing game might be evolved.

In 1920 I heard Arthur Nikisch, for the last time, in
Amsterdam. He had not been heard in England after
1914, and soon afterwards he died. He asked for the
Schumann D minor Symphony, and began with a down
beat, then nothing more until a gentle turn to the second
violins (on his right, of course) indicated the start of their
phrase on the fourth quaver of the second bar. He was
showing at the outset that he was not interested in
beating time, he was conducting the music.

There were occasional stops and modifications, though
he always avoided stopping where possible; he would
wait for a silence or a pause and then gather up two or
three points which might have cropped up since the last
stop. So all went very smoothly until the exciting silence

which comes before the *presto* at the end of the last move-ment. He held this silence a long time, and then with a stage-whispered 'Eins, zwei', he led the basses off on their torrent of quavers, with sparks flying out of the point of his stick, and the music flared up into a blaze of brilliance which excited the orchestra so that they couldn't resist a cheer at the end. Nikisch had taken their measure; he knew he could whip up the tension in a moment, but he had no need to do this in any subsequent rehearsal: it could be relied on at the performance.

At the other end of the scale we have the practice of most American conductors (whose rehearsal time is always generous) who start the first rehearsal at a hundred per cent tension, and go on through the whole period, insisting on perfection in every bar, and knocking off every time they detect the slightest lapse from com-plete perfection. A member of the B.B.C. Orchestra told me that a very eminent American who conducted *The Rite of Spring* in Queen's Hall had not allowed them to play ten bars in succession, even at the final rehearsal. He could trust his temperament to give the necessary sweep to the performance, but I don't think many of us could.

Is it an over-simplification to say that these two methods are suited to different national temperaments, and that both have their value according to nationality? I am quite certain that Nikisch's method is right for the Anglo-Saxon, and I think I would add the Dutchman and the Scandinavian, perhaps also the North German. The sport-loving Britisher surely responds well to the customs of sporting training; everything starts in moderation and the tension is gradually increased, until the clever trainer has the team at the top of their form and masters of their

Arthur Nikisch.

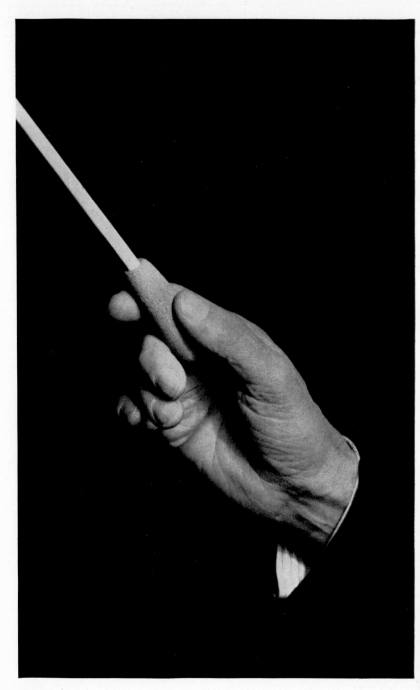

The grasp of the stick.

technical skill on the great day itself. It was said of Nikisch that he never tried drastically to alter the fundamental style of the musicians he met; he simply moulded it, in the most important respects, to his way of seeing the music, and never strained his rehearsal time to the limit. The available time, or most of it, was used to affirm the most important things, and the players could then be trusted to apply what he said to similar and parallel passages.

I have not enough experience to be able to assert that the more southern and eastern temperaments need a tighter rein than this. There is no doubt that they usually get it, and in America, where the personnel of most orchestras includes very few members of Anglo-Saxon descent, the unlimited rehearsal time, the elevation of the conductor to the position held by the *prima donna* in the nineteenth century, the tendency to keep the orchestral musician in a place of complete subservience, and not to encourage even the orchestra soloists to play passages their own way, is almost universal. The result has its advantages. Our critics always comment on the fabulous *ensemble*, but sometimes deplore the streamlining and chromium plating in the performances of visitors from over the Atlantic. We can take our choice, but I don't think a compromise is possible.

Working with a famous American orchestra with the usual generous rehearsal schedule, I thought I would content myself with a general run through the whole programme at the first rehearsal, and I then should be able to plan the other sessions in a balanced way. We naturally met some difficult passages on the first morning, for a good deal of the music was new to the players. I then started the second rehearsal with the most difficult work, which I expected to find somewhat improved since the day before. In similar circumstances British players would have taken the parts home and practised them a bit, and they would have needed very little more work on them after that. However, this time it sounded no better, and I am afraid I let loose some such sarcasm as, 'That passage doesn't seem to have benefited by its night's rest; do you want me to play it through slowly and pull it to pieces?' I am very glad to say that my bad temper was completely lost on the distinguished foreigner who was leading the orchestra, who responded with an eager 'Oh yes, please'. Well, that is all right, I suppose, when you have a whole week to rehearse one programme, but I'm afraid I prefer the British way.

In this country of strictly limited rehearsal time it is of vital importance that one should sketch beforehand a plan of how the precious time is to be spent. Things don't always go just as one hopes, and for this reason I always try to plan for a two-and-a-half-hour total, so that if one needs the extra half-hour it is there, and if not, everyone will be pleased and fresher when the time of the concert comes. Personally I have a phobia about keeping people hanging about. Accordingly I rehearse when possible in diminishing order like Haydn's 'Farewell'. Luckily it usually works out that the piece which employs the biggest orchestra is the most modern and difficult, and therefore obviously comes first—equally obviously a string work will be taken last, and when it is the Mahler *Adagietto* it is just too bad that the harp has had to wait all that time. I am afraid I can't believe the story of the temperamental visitor who spotted the absence of the third trumpet. After a complaint and a discussion with the orchestral manager it is discovered that the third trumpet has gone to the wrong hall and will be along in half an hour. An interval is called, and when they all duly re-assemble half an hour later plus the lost third trumpet, the distinguished visitor says he will rehearse the Mozart string Serenade!

Mr Neville Cardus has recently described how Beecham in rehearsal seemed to be sitting back, enjoying the sounds he was hearing, and only rarely leading the charge with the point of his stick. This is another aspect of the practice of Nikisch which we have been examining. At rehearsals one must remember to listen the whole time—it is surprising what one can miss if one starts getting caught up by the sound and tries to 'drive the engine' as if it were already the performance. In the early stages particularly, I am sure it is wise to leave things alone as far as possible and reserve comments until one's observations have crystallized any faults into one or two general points which one can ask the players to remedy through-out, without worrying each time they crop up. I'm sure we conductors talk too much. I often find that after playing a work straight through and then perhaps making three or four general comments, I can repeat a few relevant passages, and if time is short trust the players to apply these points to the rest of the work.

It is not too easy, when one knows that one has to accomplish in three hours the preparation of a pro-gramme that deserves nine or twelve, to preserve a cheerful exterior, and set a rehearsal atmosphere that will get the best work out of our colleagues in the shortest possible time; but this is what we all must learn, and I would repeat again a word as to the avoidance of too much stopping. Of course the conductor goes to his first rehearsal with a vision of an ideal performance, but he cannot expect to achieve this in the first few moments. Wisdom will suggest that he listens to what is going on, and when he reaches the end, or a pause, or a silence, he can go back over all the points, moulding what is in front of him gradually and gently in the direction of his ideal. It is not hard to keep a list of this kind in one's head, and when six points are dealt with at once instead of stopping for each one a good deal of time and irritation can be saved, and the conductor will probably finish much nearer his ideal than if he had tried instantly to impose it. I have frequently observed Nikisch and Toscanini rehearsing in this manner.

I feel, too, in this connection that with a new work first impressions are of great importance. Now if this first impression is a string of short bursts punctuated by long dissertations on tonal balance, technique, colour, or anything else, the result in the mind of the player will hardly contribute to the long view and continuous sweep of a fine performance. The architecture of a work is of fundamental importance—so fundamental that it should be made clear to everyone at the outset, and left so firmly in the mind of the player that he conveys it of necessity— even if unconsciously—to the audience. This becomes an impossibility if every bar has to be closely examined before anyone knows how the work is going to end.

There may sometimes be points of style that are better settled at the outset; the opening figure of the *allegro* of the Schubert 'Great C major', for instance, is worth stopping over at once, to get its bowing fixed once and for all. I remember many years ago a distinguished guest conductor spending the first eighteen minutes of a rehearsal worrying over a difficult *arpeggio* in bar six of a work. The section of the orchestra concerned with the *arpeggio* consisted mostly of some fairly hard-boiled old hands, whose attitude to the work, to the conductor, and to life in general was considerably soured by the experience; and a few shy girls, who were so petrified with fright that their contributions to the performance were reduced to something infinitesimal. The disastrous psychological effect of this was not remedied until the great man had gone home three days later.

Good rehearsing and good teaching have much in common—they are, after all, fundamentally identical. The teacher, or conductor, must stimulate the individual to think for himself, feel for himself, and react instantly to what others round him are doing and feeling. In this way a team spirit can gradually emerge.

Gustav Holst once said that long experience of teaching had taught him that it was impossible to be angry without also being funny. I never saw him funny because he was angry; he had a great personal dignity which I should think made this almost impossible, but it is a valuable maxim for the rehearser. Another is to avoid the word 'don't' whenever possible. It is usually easy to turn the request round constructively and ask for the passage to be more so-and-so. Positive requests are much pleasanter to hear (and receive) than their negative counterparts.

Many problems of style crop up at rehearsals, and their solution must often be personal—executants have different ideas of style and must express things as they feel them. I should, however, like to point to one rhythmical figure which is so constantly heard wrongly that it is worth discussing. How rarely is a crotchet following a minim in 3-time or following a dotted minim in 4 given its full length or its full weight!

The same of course applies to a quaver after a crotchet

or a dotted crotchet. The smaller note is almost always a fraction late (and therefore a fraction too short) and a fraction quieter (therefore interrupting the flow of the passage). To neglect the small notes in this way is right for Russian music but wrong for the classics. If one simply counts out loud 1, 2, 3, 4 while the passage is being played one can see clearly that 4 comes off badly in both respects. Indeed at some point (but not all the time) a magnifying glass wants to be put over the beginning and end of every note; has it, or should it have, a sharp edge, or accent, or should it carry something of a bulge, a slight *crescendo* or a *diminuendo*? Should it finish abruptly, or should it die away?

The conductor has usually to decide some question of position before his rehearsal begins. The plan of a platform or rehearsal room can present many problems. I have heard it said that the ideal positioning for an orchestra would be to let them sit with their friends exactly as they pleased. If this might work for an orchestra it certainly wouldn't for a chorus! Chorus members are too fond of conversation. But the fact is that there is no perfect way—there are always disadvantages, and without examining a number of fancy plans which have been seen and heard from time to time, I think we can agree on some general points. I would always place the woodwind first on a platform; the four soloists together in the very middle; and the others radiating outwards in two rows. Next perhaps the horns, usually to the left (from the conductor's viewpoint) of the woodwind, but not too near a side or back wall, for their tone emerges behind them, and will be powerfully thrown back if the wall is too close. This can happen in the Royal Festival Hall if the wooden fence which separates chorus and orchestra is too near. The other brass can usually go on the right, and I like trombones to play rather at an angle towards the middle and not straight down the hall. Their tone will blend better in that way. I like the string basses in a row at the back, Vienna-fashion, but in many halls it is impossible and they have to go away in some corner. This is unfortunate; the string foundation should be central, and I can remember Hans Richter, who had eight, placing four in each corner of the platform. He felt it better to separate them than to leave the tone unbalanced.

This brings us to the other strings. In the last thirty years world opinion has swung right over to a separation of the strings according to pitch; all the treble is on the left and all the bass on the right. I find this most disagreeable, for instance, in the Royal Festival Hall, where it is quite possible to hear the bass tone ahead of the violin tone and therefore more prominent, because if one sits on the extreme right the violins are so much farther away. It is therefore in my view essential that a proper balance between first and second violins be secured by placing the seconds on the conductor's right, so that the treble of the string sound reaches the audience from the whole width of the front of the platform. This must have been in Rimsky-Korsakov's mind when he wrote the slow movement of *Scheherazade*.

Until recently, when I was accepting a guest engagement I usually left the platform plan alone, but the almost complete extinction of the second violins when they are placed beside and (more usually) behind the firsts, has caused me nowadays to insist on this balance wherever I am. It is argued that the second violins cannot be heard so well when the bridges of their instruments are on the inward side; this is only true if they sit hunched up with their backs to the audience. If they sit squarely on the platform facing the conductor, no one who shuts his eyes and really listens can possibly think that they are in a weaker position on the right. Further, in almost every symphonic work from Mozart to Elgar can be found passages where the two violin groups answer each other phrase by phrase—these are completely ineffective when the reply is a pale reflection coming from the depths behind the firsts instead of asserting itself from the front of the platform. I have said that Hans Richter's practice was usually to divide his double basses in order to achieve a balance; he would have been horrified if anyone had asked him to let all his violins sit together on his left.

The right-hand position for second violins puts a considerable strain on the first desk in regard to *ensemble*, particularly when there is a piano on the platform to separate them still farther from the first violins. But I find that players enjoy the challenge and I have very rarely had to complain of slackness in that quarter.

There is little to be said about the rest of the players; they can be fitted in according to the space available— usually not over-generous, and demanding some compromise and some discomfort somewhere. The perfect platform is rare, and of course conditions must vary according to the size of the orchestra, the presence of a chorus, and so on. In regard to choruses, numerical weakness of the men nowadays often demands a closely packed centre with the tenors well forward. The stronger ranks of women stretch out each side as the platform allows.

A word here is necessary on the height of the box on which the conductor is mounted. If two players are sharing music at one desk, they will both find their music and the conductor's field of gesture separated from each other by a slight angle. It follows that the angle should be as small as possible and the same for each player; a capital letter Y represents these lines of sight, with the conductor at the base of the letter, the music at the central fork, and the two players at the top points. It follows also that if the conductor has climbed up to a position four feet or more above the level of the main parts of the platform, his front players will see his knees just over their music, and will have to jerk their heads up whenever they need to see the stick. In particular the leading desks can have a miserable time glancing up at vital moments when a conductor is skied up above them. As I stand I like to feel my desk is only a few inches above the eye-level of the players. Farther back they can dovetail (or is it 'stagger'?) the positions of their heads and a close contact will be secured. Please, conductors, don't think you get more authority by standing on the top of three or four boxes. You get less, however fine it may feel. In the same way, you should see that players don't place their music so low that they have to look away to see the beat. The finest orchestral soloists I know always sit so that I can see their eyes (and perhaps their noses—never more than this) over their desks. It gives me great confidence to see this, and I know at once that there is a real sense of contact.

Dr Klemperer has always stood on the same level as his seated players; but then he measures, I believe, about six feet six in height. We lesser mortals must be high enough to exercise control, but if the string players' positions are properly staggered most of us can do best with platforms of not more than a foot in height, certainly never more than two feet, however short we are.

THOUGHTS ON CONDUCTING

In these days of scarcity of halls, and the consequent congestion in their use, it is often necessary to hold preliminary rehearsals in small rooms of painful inadequacy. The players will all be on one level, and may have great difficulty in hearing anyone but their next neighbour. There is one point here which the conductor must be firm about; his position must be as far as possible from the principal window; it is quite impossible for players to follow a beat or read their music when there is a strong light in front of them. When I go to a meeting and find the chairman's place, as so often, nearest the window with his back to the light, I know at once that he is either selfish or incompetent—perhaps both! The same is true of a conductor in a rehearsal room.

Intonation, as is well known, creates a great number of problems. It is impossible to hope for perfect tuning throughout the varied kinds and sizes of instruments which make up a full orchestra unless everyone has it in mind all through every rehearsal and performance. Some listeners' ears are so sensitive that they hear beats in every orchestral sound; a former poet laureate (Robert Bridges), for instance, was said only to get real pleasure from music for unaccompanied choir, for this could give the most perfect intonation possible to human beings.

This difficulty, and many others, can often be met satisfactorily by means of split rehearsals; wind and percussion together; and then strings. Technical problems of string playing particularly can be tackled without the feeling that the wind players are wasting their time, and from the contractual point of view it can be a great saving; for each player only works for three hours while the conductor—and possibly the librarian—work for six.

It may sometimes be useful to delegate the string

rehearsal to the leader. He has probably spent some time marking the bowings and fingerings in the parts and may well enjoy an hour or two coaching the result of his work. It prevents his playing himself, of course, but I don't think this matters.

I am often asked just what the leader has to do in an orchestra. He is responsible for the uniform bowing and fingering of difficult passages, and at a first reading of a new work his example helps the rank and file with the tackling of difficult passages. After the early rehearsal stage he appears to melt into the *ensemble*, though his vigilance is to be seen the moment anything appears to go wrong. As the audience well knows, he represents the orchestra at the beginning of the concert. At any moment he may have to intervene if psychological blunders are being committed by a conductor at rehearsal, and he is normally accepted as deputy conductor if necessary.

It is often worth considering whether to rehearse a work at exactly its performing speed. Our continental friends, who must have a concert going on all through every rehearsal, will obviously never allow themselves to make any variation, except when absolutely necessary for interludes devoted to mastering difficult passages. Nikisch, on the other hand, often at a final rehearsal in front of a packed Gewandhaus, would linger over some phrase, and exaggerate its nuance, just to let it drop into place in exact proportion when the performance came. To take a little more time over an *allegro* than your final intention will often save a great deal of rehearsal time; things that are not quite right will often show clearly that they are going to be 'all right next time', and can be left without further fuss. Fast movements of the *scherzo* type will often benefit from rehearsal at a pace slightly faster than the final *tempo*. If one finds that it is too much of a scramble, a steadier performance will automatically clear things up, but if it 'works' at an excessive speed in the right kind of hall, with the right kind of orchestra and choir, well then, perhaps on this occasion the performance can also take it, with brilliant results!

Years ago, talking about the *scherzo* of the Vaughan Williams *London Symphony*, I said that I felt it wanted to go faster than I had been rehearsing it. Geoffrey Toye, who conducted the first performance of the work, said: 'No, Adrian, it just won't go any faster than that.' Somehow its pace on paper seems faster than it is possible to play it. The composer, who said it should go 'as quickly as possible', did not himself force the pace unduly.

There are a number of special problems concerned with amateurs in rehearsal. In general one can assume that amateurs have a wider general scope of interest than professionals, and can take allusions of a nature that might well bore a professional. In my very young days I remember a conductor, whose most successful career had been built up mainly with amateurs, looking up at the stodgiest possible row of professional double-bass players (many of them used to wear bowler hats at rehearsals) and saying: 'Gentlemen, please let it sound like the loveliest gauze.' I looked under the bowler hats to see whether any inspiration had emanated from the exhortation, but I saw very little sign of it.

There is a real fascination in work with amateurs; they give back the conductor's enthusiasm with interest, and I find it most stimulating. I was conductor of the Bach Choir (which meant absolute regularity at the weekly practices; they have never had a chorus-master) when I went to the B.B.C. in 1930, and I often felt when five o'clock came round after a tiring office day that I had no business to go off and get a fee for rehearsing people when I felt so flat; but ten minutes after the rehearsal had started I had been refreshed by the keenness of the choir. I was later only reluctantly forced to give it up because regularity of attendance became impossible.

In rehearsing amateurs it is important to make a plan, not only for each rehearsal as we have recommended for professionals, but also for the series of rehearsals culminating in the concert. I sang for a short and valuable time in the Oriana Madrigal Society with that great choralist Charles Kennedy Scott. He printed a rehearsal schedule; he knew exactly how long everything would take, and always stuck to it. I don't think it is necessary that members should all have a copy, but if they don't it is wise for the conductor to drop a hint now and then as to its existence. If every member realizes that something vital is in hand at every rehearsal he will be less likely to accept an outside invitation for the practice night.

If I had, say, ten rehearsals for a work, I should devote the major part of perhaps six or seven of them to learning fresh work. This would occupy at least half of each rehearsal, and should start each week, unless a few minutes' deep breathing and tonal exercises might come before. Recapitulation of previous work should always be touched on later, and the rehearsal should finish with some enjoyable singing of parts that are already well known. If the recapitulation goes badly, a nice opportunity presents itself for something of this sort: 'Well, we don't seem to have really learnt this properly yet. Let me see—I think I noticed one or two empty chairs in the sopranos when we got down to learning it last week.

Perhaps a little private study could repair the gap before next week.'

In large choirs it is very important that the whole body should be equally familiar with the work in hand, and this is not easy to secure. There are bound to be some good readers and the others are bound to depend on them. It is quite a good idea to try a passage without the front row, or invent some kind of trick to see how *everyone* is getting on. It need not be a bad thing for the choir if the rehearsal pianist is not too good at his job. This sounds hard-hearted to the conductor, but it is true that a choir that is led by an eager pianist is not going to learn so thoroughly. When teaching elementary choirs and children it is most unwise to hammer their parts on the piano, or sing them loudly, while they sing, for it goes into their ears and straight out of their mouths. The phrases should be patterned by voice, violin, or piano, and then sung by the choir. In this way there is much more chance of retention; they have had to hear and retain it before reproducing it, and the two processes are separate.

It is not at all necessary to conduct the whole time in these early stages; in fact I evolved a 'heads down, heads up' practice with the Birmingham Festival Choir, and often played the piano myself, so that while learning they could concentrate on the music, and when they knew it they could hold their copies well up and see the beat above them. This was another thing I learnt from Nikisch. He always rehearsed the Gewandhaus Choir himself, sitting at the piano on the platform of the chamber music hall. We men sat round him, with the women and boys of Bach's St Thomas's Church in the body of the hall. Though he always had the full score on the piano and played from it, he rarely conducted, though one of his sticks lay on the piano desk. We hardly ever saw him conduct until the orchestral rehearsals, when we were ready to follow his beat.

Regarding amateur *orchestras*, the most troublesome aspect is their incompleteness. Personally I feel that it is much better to have too many players than too few, and if I see five or six clarinet players sitting together, I invite them all to play all the time, except perhaps for a few bars of absolute solo. Another problem for the conductor of amateurs is the fact that on some instruments an inexperienced player will play very loudly in order to secure his note; on some others he will be so discreet that he becomes inaudible. I used to have a thrilling time in Oxford days sitting at the piano with a full score at the weekly rehearsals of Sir Hugh Allen's orchestra. It was nearly complete—often only six or eight professionals would be engaged for the concert—but I could help in various ways and I learnt a great deal.

4

Accompaniment and Orchestral Balance

I HAVE a feeling that many conductors (and orchestras) are inclined to think that a concerto is a somewhat unwelcome interruption to a concert, stuck in
just to help the box office, and needing an unfair amount
of rehearsal time, because nearly every soloist in the world
wants to play through every note of the concerto on the
day of the concert, even if he or she has played it the day
before.

I am afraid I don't agree at all. To begin with it alters
the balance of responsibility in the concert. A concert
consisting of three string quartets (or two if they are long
ones) is a perfect kind of programme, and, likewise, a
series of two or three symphonies or other orchestral
masterpieces wonderfully performed can give us a
memorable evening; but the average orchestral concert
can gain very much from the contrast of a fine concerto
finely performed. Some of them get hackneyed because
they are a good draw, but far too few of the Mozart

Toscanini.

Toscanini conducting the B.B.C. Symphony Orchestra, 1935.

pianoforte concertos, for instance, are well known, and many others, rarely if ever heard, are also masterpieces.

A very distinguished soloist told me recently that in America he often found himself relegated to the last forty minutes of the last rehearsal (there had perhaps been three or four), when conductor and orchestra quite obviously wanted to get away to lunch. This procedure gives the poor soloist no chance to say whether he wants anything special with regard to *tempo* or anything else. He must just give one more average performance, poor creature.

Personally I dare say I overdo it, but whenever possible I meet the soloist beforehand and give him a chance to tell me exactly what he wants. This may sometimes involve a word or two to the orchestra before the actual rehearsal of the concerto, but it seems to me the only fair way of handling the whole thing. A very keen listener in my B.B.C. days once said he was always amused to hear the differences we used to make in the introductory *ritornello* of a concerto to conform with what the soloist was going to do later in the movement.

One sometimes hears stories of classical concerto performances at which conductor and soloist have agreed to differ, and the soloist has his way in the solos, but at every *tutti* the orchestra would jump forwards, or drag backwards, and maintain this change until the next solo entry. This is a nice way to present a great classic to a long-suffering audience! In the opera house it is different: the various moods and temperaments of the singers and the parts they play must be co-ordinated by someone, and that someone is obviously the conductor; but in the concert hall it is surely a pleasant contrast for all concerned to let the interpretative initiative pass from the conductor to someone else for part of the time, and sheer sportsmanship surely should allow the soloist to have his way for half an hour when the conductor is the unquestioned boss for the rest of the concert. I think it may usually be assumed that the soloist has spent a hundred hours practising and thinking about the concerto to every one spent by the conductor, so presumably the soloist does know best.

It might be amusing to recount an experience of mine which is, I think, the most extreme example in my memory of a difference with a soloist. In the early years of the B.B.C. Symphony Orchestra we always offered our soloist two rehearsals, the first with pianoforte or with orchestra, as he wished. The second was, of course, with orchestra, but on this occasion Gieseking, whose visits were always looked forward to by us all with great pleasure, arrived literally at the eleventh hour on the morning of the concert. He had been playing in Holland the night before. He came on to the platform of the old Queen's Hall and looked with horror at the assembled array of something like seventy string players waiting to play the Bach D minor Concerto, which I had always looked on, and played with others, as a robust, vigorous, open-air kind of piece. In reply to his question I said that the players did know how to accompany, and suggested we should try a movement and see what he thought. At the end of the movement he still thought there were too many, and though the balance engineer and I both assured him that the tone of the pianoforte showed clearly above the strings, he said he found the texture was wrong. The word 'texture' struck me, and I said: 'Mr Gieseking, are you really thinking of this as a pianoforte concerto, or one with harpsichord?' He jumped at once and said, yes, he was thinking of the harpsichord all the time, although he had to play on the enormous concert grand that had been provided for him. I thereupon sent about fifty of the orchestra home, and the other twenty stayed and tinkled through the concerto to Gieseking's satisfaction. He asked me afterwards whether I hadn't liked it so, and I had to confess that I had always thought this concerto a more robust work, but that I was very happy that our audience and listeners should have the opportunity of hearing a different point of view. Gieseking was a very great pianist indeed, and his conception, though different from the one usually held, was logical and may well have been nearer to the performances which Bach himself gave.

I'm afraid I am rather a rebel about the feeling that people seem to have, that if an orchestral accompaniment is too strong, the removal of a few strings will improve matters. I can't agree; you may get a clearer picture of the woodwind if you do this, but you will certainly have too much brass, unless you warn the players very firmly; and if it is a violin concerto you will be bringing your *tutti* violin tone that much nearer to a solo quality. Provided that they will play quietly, the contrast will be greater, and the tone more beautiful the greater the number of players taking part. Berlioz has said that one instrument alone can be beautiful; two, playing the same tune, far less so, but after that as the number increases the beauty also can increase, and I would add that this is true both in *pianissimo* and *fortissimo*: the more people you have playing the same tune, the more beautiful it is, whether loud or soft. This applies equally to prominent passages and accompaniments, provided that every player really plays softly when required, and listens, as he plays, to whatever line is most important.

THOUGHTS ON CONDUCTING

There is no doubt that the inner parts of Mozart's *fortes* show more clearly when the strings are reduced, and I don't often feel like doubling the woodwind to make them show; but a good deal can be done with care and ample rehearsal.

Another problem about which I feel pretty strongly is where to stand in a pianoforte concerto. For some reason in this country (very rarely anywhere else, I believe) the conductor often takes his place between the instrument and the audience. This has many drawbacks; the conductor will have to be mounted uncomfortably high, and we have seen how awkward this can be for the front desks of strings, and even then he will find the piano lid in the way of his contact with the orchestra and in danger of its breaking his stick for him. Certain of my more unscrupulous colleagues arrange for the stick which supports the piano lid to be shortened somewhat. This upsets the angle chosen by the maker to reflect the sound straight into the hall; with a short stick the sound is thrown at the feet of the people in the front row of the stalls. No, a short stick is most unfair to the soloists, whose tone will be misdirected and muffled. Moreover, the most serious objection to the conductor's being in that position is that he has the whole weight of the piano tone just under his nose and ears, and cannot possibly judge accurately whether the orchestra is drowning the soloist. I had my final lesson on this point many years ago when I had the pleasure of conducting a performance of the Second Rachmaninoff played by a brilliant young musician named Malcolm Sargent. The rehearsal had gone well, I thought, and after the orchestra had dispersed for tea I was approached by a gentleman who had been listening. 'Excuse me, Mr Boult', he said, 'but I think I ought to tell you that I haven't heard much of the piano this afternoon.' Hasty injunctions had to be passed to the brass before the concert, but I vowed from then on to take my place in a concerto behind the instrument and near the orchestra so that I could hear what they were doing. I can't pretend it is comfortable there; I place my desk close by the keyboard and in line with it, so that in the solos I can watch the keyboard and my music (if I need it) together. For *tutti* I turn more centrally to the orchestra, hoping I don't need the score much, but in both solos and *tutti* I have to be careful that the stick is moving in a central plane, so that the leader of the orchestra and the leader of the second violins can both see it all the time. The piano must, of course, be pushed as near the edge of the platform as possible to make room for me.

So we are going to give our soloists their heads (even if they lose them) and take our place behind the piano. We must also take care to keep our key sense (if we haven't got absolute pitch) through the most elaborate *cadenza* if we don't want to get caught napping at the end, and I am always most grateful to the soloist who gives me a copy of it. Very few of them do, I am afraid.

I must defer to a number of more scholarly works which discuss the performance of seventeenth-century music, and, in particular, the *continuo* and its realization. The choice between harpsichord, pianoforte, and organ, the addition of one or two string basses and cellos, are all matters of importance, and however our conductor decides between the experts, all will agree that the result must be a beautiful sound that makes balanced sense and expresses the feeling of the poetry and the music in a way which can reach and touch the audience.

I was brought up in the time of mammoth performances of Bach and Handel, so I am not so horrified
by them as some people are nowadays. I like small-scale
performances too, but cannot believe that the 'Crucifixus'
or 'Qui tollis' can ever sound so moving with a choir of
forty as they do with two hundred people, all of whom
are listening to the flutes as they sing. Strangely, the
'Sanctus' can sound most impressive with a small
balanced choir and orchestra.

Recitatives may conveniently be dealt with in this
chapter; we meet them in concerts as well as in opera.
Most oratorio parts are printed with the voice part shown
parallel to the string part, and this seems to remove
from the conductor some of his responsibility, for the
players can hardly help watching the voice part and
following it as they play. I feel, however, that no conductor should trade on this, and I am always most careful
to show the players every bar line, and without necessarily giving a precise gesture for every beat, showing
them always the rise of each bar to the bar line, and its
fall at that point, as we have described earlier. Singers
often take great liberties, but there is usually a stan-
dardization which can be learned beforehand at a piano
rehearsal. It is important to get to know the music
itself very well indeed; by heart in fact. This is true of all
accompaniments. If anything goes wrong it can nearly
always be found to consist purely and simply in the
conductor's failure to know, really to know, the music.
Learn your music; you can never know it too well.

My practice then, where accompaniments are concerned, is to sink myself as far as possible into the soloists'
conception of the work, and I find I much enjoy adapting
my view to what they feel about it. It is surprising that it

is not always easy to find out what they do feel; they can be sharply divided into two schools. My practice with strangers, if it has been impossible to arrange a private rehearsal with piano, is to ask them to play or sing at the rehearsal exactly how they wish to perform at the concert; if I don't conform at once we can make an adjustment as soon as possible. Accordingly, soon after I start the orchestral introduction which usually precedes their entry, I ask whether the pace is right. Some soloists will answer this decisively and helpfully, and I can then make an adjustment, if necessary, so that the *tempo* is right when they come in. Others will look horrified, and either say they don't know yet, or make some reply which turns out, as soon as they make their entry, to have been quite wrong. It is often not until the movement is over that I can find out how it should start, and sometimes, worse still, those who have begun their careers with a few years' orchestral work and cannot help following the beat even when they disagree with it, will play through to the end, and then timidly ask whether it could all be a little slower or faster. I am afraid I have the greatest difficulty in preventing an explosion at this maddening waste of rehearsal time when I have already told them to play at their own pace so that I can do it their way. However, one has patiently to start again, though time often won't allow a replay of the complete movement.

5

Opera and Ballet

THERE is a very healthy operatic life in this country, and excellent performances are often heard not only of the lighter things that we in England feel are especially our province, but more serious things as well. Professional opera can be divided into two groups. There is the hand-to-mouth type of operatic festival, where an experienced and distinguished company is collected and let loose with a minimum of rehearsal, held together by a clever conductor with a first-rate (we hope) orchestra. Or, what is now the general rule even here, the work of a repertory company which builds up its new production through weeks of preparatory work, the conductor of the opera concerned himself coaching soloists and chorus, and giving precise instructions to staff men as to how this is to be done. Finally, he gathers the strands together, as it were, until everything fits in as he has envisaged it, and the performance goes with a swing.

There is, however, one technical point which I would stress, and this is often overlooked. There is a strong light on the conductor's score, and the light reflected from this score shows up noticeably the conductor's shirt front and usually his face. Here he can make his stick a really telling instrument so that the orchestra sees the underside of it. Even the back of the stage can usually see it in that lighted space. There is therefore no need at all for him to wave about in the dark over his head in the hope that part of the message may get somewhere. Nikisch at Covent Garden in 1914 hardly lifted his hand above the level of his face right through *The Ring*.

There are obviously many conflicting and contrasting factors which must be brought together to make a complete operatic performance, and it is often a difficult task which only rarely can be solved by a despotic exercise of power, usually by the conductor, sometimes by the producer. It is often a matter of interplay of personalities, and give and take, once the right people are cast for the singing roles, designs, dresses, and musical equipment; under sympathetic guidance it is astonishing how much beauty and understanding can be brought into the service of the work. I think, however, that the reigns of Toscanini at Milan, Mahler in Vienna, Walter at Munich, prove that the greatest operatic performances have to emanate from a single mind.

In the early twenties I attended a rehearsal at Munich of *Figaro*. Walter used to say that he played it every three weeks all the year round, and always had a three-hour rehearsal in the morning. The first hour was spent on recitatives, and later the orchestra came and they rehearsed *ensembles*. Whenever Walter stopped he would start them again by singing somebody's part—he never referred to a section letter or bar number, but might accompany the singer on his harpsichord for a bar or two, and everybody had joined in by then. I never heard a rehearsal anywhere else where everybody taking part knew the work by heart. In the earlier part of the rehearsal Walter was on the stage, and someone else played the recitatives for him. He was continually polishing matters of diction and position, but when he felt he was moving the singers about too much he would come to the front of the stage and say, 'Sie erlauben, Herr Professor' ('Permit me'). Out of the darkness of the back row of the stalls a shadowy figure could just be seen to bow his assent. This was the producer, who evidently knew his place when Bruno Walter was in command!

I have had very little experience of ballet since I was pitchforked into a Diaghileff season at three days' notice in 1919. There was naturally no opportunity until after we had started to visit the ballet room and to learn the way the dance and the music coalesced, and I found that the great difficulty about remembering the *tempo* of music which I hadn't known beforehand (nearly all of it) was that I had the dancers at my mercy; they were quite unable to show me what they wanted, as any singer or soloist can do—in fact does sometimes involuntarily. They could only tell me after it was all over, and so we come round to the previous rule: Learn your music; you can never know it too well.

I imagine that the modern dancer is less at the mercy of the conductor than the Russians forty years ago, and the amazing rise of the Royal Ballet under Dame Ninette de Valois's inspiring direction has evolved an art very different from that which indeed produced some fine results under Diaghileff's despotic rule. I have some very happy recollections of performances, especially Vaughan Williams's *Job*, with this wonderful company.

6

Performance

THE great day has come, and we are keyed up for the
ordeal. I am sometimes asked what happens if I go
to a concert feeling that I want to do a Beethoven
symphony, and I find a Tchaikovsky on the programme.
My reply is that that kind of attitude is the privilege
of the amateur; the professional has several days before
(much longer if it is something involving fresh preparation) begun to condition himself for a performance of a
Tchaikovsky symphony. He has thought through it on
waking in the early morning, he has planned his rehearsal
when sitting in the Underground, and he has pictured the
orchestra waiting for rehearsal in the hall while standing
in a bus queue. Is he nervous? Of course he is; if I hear an
artist saying that he is never nervous, I know at once he is
one of those technically slick people whose performance
will move no one at all except his relations. Or possibly
he is like a friend of mine who suffered acutely and was
persuaded to take a very useful homoeopathic remedy
before a concert, with this lamentable result: 'My dear, I

can never take it again; I found myself positively revelling in playing wrong notes!' Nerves are sent to stimulate us to do more than our best, and must be welcomed, and harnessed to help our work whether at a concert or before an athletic ordeal.

How else do we prepare ourselves? I for one found it a great mistake to give way to the feeling we all have—that food is impossible before a concert. My experience is that if I starve before a concert (as one naturally wants to) I shall be so hungry by half time that I shall be worn out and useless by the end of the programme. I find, too, that it is most harmful to get to the hall too early; artists' rooms are poisonous places—their wallpapers exude noxious thoughts. I still often walk to concerts if the distance is reasonable, and I time myself to get there not too long beforehand; sometimes I go out again if I have got there too soon. I have sometimes been amused at the consternation in the faces of members of the audience when they meet their conductor walking rapidly away from the hall only a few minutes before the start of the concert.

We have discussed the method of preparation and the pros and cons for the generation of tension at rehearsals; I repeat that I prefer the cooler method, gradually warming up (provided rehearsals are plentiful), so that the peak of excitement is just reached, but not passed, when the audience is in the hall and the performance begins.

One stands in the doorway looking out on the orchestra, and hoping that one can get to the desk without knocking down half the players on the way. It all looks a very long way off, and I often have to repress a strong urge to run at full speed in order to get there—or perhaps to run harder still in the other direction. But that, as we saw, is the privilege of the amateur. Some brave spirits manage to walk on to the platform carrying their sticks, but my advice is to leave the stick on the desk, and not to pick it up until everything is ready for the music. Sticks have a very shaky habit before the music begins. So we try to stand absolutely still, looking round at our forces to see that they are all there and 'sitting comfortably' while that wonderful sound of *diminuendo* comes from the audience to convey that they too are feeling a growing expectation, and the first silence invites us to start. Now we can give up all our rehearsal cares; we shall hear all we need to hear, but our task has become that of engine driver; we supply the motive power, keeping our eye on the track with an occasional thought for danger signals, yet mainly possessed with the relentless flow of the sound to its climax and thence to its inevitable close.

There is a great variety in the *tempo* set by different conductors, not only of the music, but of the concert itself. I am an impatient person. I hate the breaks between the acts of a play, and I feel strongly the link (even when musically it is undiscernible) between the movements of a concerto or symphony. I know it is necessary, but when a violinist after closing a movement in, say, E flat major, plunges us into the D and A tuning fifth, I always feel like breaking my stick over his head. It is the custom for some conductors to leave the platform after every item—I can't think why. Of course we should go to meet a soloist, but otherwise I see no reason for going and coming any more than for a recitalist to go away between the items of his programme.

Some conductors, who seem to enjoy dawdling through their programmes, apparently take an opposite view where the length of the music itself is concerned; they cut every repeat they can find, even sometimes in *scherzos* and trios. It is perhaps arguable that in a Mozart serenade (which may have been meant to be played while the archbishop was having supper) the repeats are formally and thoughtlessly put in to fill the time up, but this is not the case with his symphonies—indeed, I now find that both repeats in the last movements of the last three symphonies are essential if those movements are to stand up to balance their great first movements. I have always found the symphonies something of a tadpole, and only recently has this most obvious reason dawned on me. Bruno Walter agreed heartily when I said I wanted to hear those repeats. It seems to be especially in the orchestral world that this omission is so often practised. In quartets and sonatas they seem to be played much more often. Of course movements vary in this necessity; for instance, in the *Eroica* I feel neutral about it—though Kleiber's recent record is published in full; but in works like the Fifth of Beethoven and the Third of Brahms I feel the movement almost headless without it.

I am afraid we still hear the expression 'seeing a conductor' used even in educated circles. Do people really spend their money in the hope of seeing a ballet or peepshow? If so, why not go to the ballet straight away (they are better trained for this than we are)? Are such people disappointed when a man stands still and uses his stick continuously and his elbows rarely? It takes all sorts to make a world. Seriously, I sometimes feel that conductors are insulting skilled orchestral colleagues not only in the way they speak at rehearsals, but by their behaviour at concerts, dotting every *i* and crossing every *t*, giving them credit for no sense or artistry, and never allowing the music to move, as it were, in its own way and sweep on to its goal. I know some of my colleagues occasionally talk about 'my Brahms' and 'your Mozart'. Can't they see that the finest praise they can get is not 'What a fine performance', but something like: 'I thought I knew and loved the work, but tonight it sounded even greater than I imagined it'?

7

Various Methods Discussed

NIKISCH

I HAVE already told how Nikisch was my first inspiration, the first conductor whom I as a young man felt to be in possession of some hitherto undisclosed secret, some method of conducting which was economical as to means and yet could attain ends as lofty and indeed as impassioned as any other style of conducting.

Here I want to enlarge upon that, by considering in closer detail Nikisch's stick technique and method of rehearsal. I feel I must put on record an impression, based on six months' close watching, of his method, particularly in the rehearsal room, for its economy and effectiveness have no equal in my experience and should not be forgotten.

To begin with, he made his stick say more than any other conductor that I have ever watched. Its power of expression was so intense that one felt it would be quite impossible, for instance, to play *staccato* when Nikisch was showing a *legato*. There was no need for him to stop

Furtwängler conducting the Vienna Philharmonic Orchestra; a concert televised from the Albert Hall, 1948.

The author with Sir Henry Wood (seated) and Basil Cameron; the 1942 season of Promenade Concerts.

and ask for a *sostenuto*—his stick had already pulled it from the players. And so on, with almost every kind of nuance. It followed, then, that a most sensitive left hand could be used (albeit most sparingly and economically) to supplement the expression shown by the stick, and so there seemed that very little was left for verbal explanation.

In the Leipzig Gewandhaus Nikisch also had the Wednesday morning public rehearsal in which to work. There was a general impression that this was exactly like the concert; in fact, rehearsal-goers used sometimes to give themselves airs, and criticize the well-dressed evening audience as fashionable and non-musical. Nikisch evidently did not subscribe to this view, for he would rehearse quite blatantly in front of the rehearsal audience. He never stopped, but with left hand and eyes would indicate, for instance, that something had been far too loud, and should be corrected at the performance. His preliminary rehearsals (which we students had the privilege of attending) would be devoted to the more out-of-the-way things on the programme. The standard classic might not be touched at all—or perhaps only a few chosen passages taken. The rest, and all concertos, were tried for the first time at the public rehearsal, a procedure not always satisfactory to the soloists!

In later life Nikisch had a curious aversion to studying scores. He was always ready to do new works, but said that he could not think out his interpretation from the cold print, but must have the living sound under his hand. I sat next to George Butterworth when Nikisch took the second rehearsal of the *Shropshire Lad* at Leeds in 1913. At the first rehearsal he had gone through it and afterwards Butterworth had asked for several slight modifications. Nikisch agreed, but did not re-rehearse then; however, ten days later he had remembered them all, and George could truthfully say that he had nothing further to suggest: the performance was exactly as he wished it.

His study methods (or lack of them) described above were once the target of that inveterate practical joker, Max Reger, who, just before Nikisch was going to start the first reading of a new work of his, shouted up from the hall: 'I say, Nikisch, may I suggest that you just run through the big double fugue before you play the work right through?' 'Certainly, my friend', was the reply. 'Gentlemen, we will begin with the big double fugue', as he turned over the pages to find it. Unfortunately there wasn't a fugue in the work at all!

It was said that the first bar of *Tristan* was enough to enable anyone to recognize blindfold the warmth and beauty of tone which unmistakably showed that Nikisch was conducting—these things cannot be described, but there is no doubt that he fully understood Wagner's axiom: that there must always be at least one singing line in any music. The power to call this up also lay in that wonderful stick, and once he knew an orchestra he would rarely demand any special tension at rehearsals. These were always peaceful, almost uneventful; only once did I see him lose his temper, and rarely did he ask for more tone—he knew that that would come when wanted, and when called for by his stick.

Another aspect of conducting in which Nikisch's practice differed from that of most of his colleagues was when he was conducting as a guest—and here too his practice seems to be near that of Toscanini. A continental newcomer conducting an orchestra for the first time usually prepares, if possible, to extract from his players a performance which coincides in every detail with the perfect performance which his imagination conjures up. In many cases this will mean total destruction of an orchestra's basic style: the possibility of a Viennese con-conductor preparing a Mahler, or even a Beethoven, symphony with a Parisian orchestra might be quoted as an example. I can also remember two disastrous rehearsals when a distinguished foreigner (whose conducting days are now over) tried to make the B.B.C. Orchestra play the *Enigma* Variations 'as Sir Elgar told us he wished in 1908'. A critic afterwards said that he seemed to have succeeded in utterly destroying the B.B.C. Orchestra's fundamental ideas of the Variations, and had evidently not had enough rehearsal time to rebuild his own con-ception on top. Nikisch would never have done this: he would simply have moulded the orchestra's normal read-ing as near to his ideal as conveniently possible in the time at his disposal.

He had a great sense of tact and contact with those with whom he was working, and M. Inghelbrecht tells in his recent book how Nikisch used to say that the mentality of different members of the orchestra varied usually with the instruments they played, and that he could speak in a subtle and delicate way to a player of the oboe or a string leader, whereas he would put the point at issue consider-ably more forcibly if he were talking, say, to the player of a heavy brass instrument.

Nikisch, as far as I know, never wrote a line about his work, so I hope that these few notes may help others, particularly those who inherit some of his genius, to profit by his experience and his practice, which are still so vividly admired by all who remember him.

What I have just said about Nikisch as a rehearser

brings other conductors to mind, and I find myself starting out on the comparative study of the various conductors I have watched at work. It is a fascinating pursuit and a valuable one as long as one focuses attention on technique and ignores (or tries to forget) personal idiosyncracies of gesture and general bearing.

TOSCANINI

One of the first conductors I should like to compare with Nikisch is Arturo Toscanini. The result of his method produced something in performance that was quite different from what Nikisch asked for and what he obtained. There was, in fact, something that made Toscanini's work different from that of every other conductor. What was it, what power was at work there?

I think the main thing about Toscanini's work was that he controlled a higher candle-power, if you like to call it that, of concentration than any human being except perhaps a few great orators. I know my father used to say that Gladstone after five minutes' speaking was absolutely dripping with perspiration, and it was the same with Toscanini after five minutes' rehearsing. And the candle-power—I can't think of anything else to call it—of concentration was so intense that nothing could interrupt it. One felt that if there had been an earthquake Toscanini would have gone on with his rehearsal.

I remember him saying: 'I never rehearse again anything that has once gone well.' This excepted of course the final rehearsal, at which he always played through the whole programme. I think it is true of all artistic matters that they can never stand still: there must always be improvement or the other thing; and where rehearsal is concerned, the moment one reaches the peak the bogy of staleness begins to rear its head. Toscanini was a most economical rehearser. He was given a generous schedule in London, it is true, but he often stopped an hour early, and he actually cancelled one or two rehearsals altogether.

It might be of interest to recall Toscanini's very first rehearsal with the B.B.C. Symphony Orchestra. It was the Brahms E minor Symphony, a work that we had played many times, I imagine, more or less in the same way. Well, when Toscanini took over he was extraordinarily sparing with his stoppings—in fact I believe the second and third movements he played straight through without a stop, and only referred afterwards to two or three points. As I have said, that is what Nikisch did. But as Toscanini played those movements, I, sitting there, was conscious that the orchestra was playing somehow in a quite different way from what they were in the habit of doing when I was conducting. Afterwards I asked a member of the orchestra why she had played that movement so differently when Toscanini was conducting. She said she didn't know, but somehow felt inevitably how he wanted the thing to go, even though it was slightly different from the way she usually played it.

Toscanini's knowledge of any score, once learnt, was complete and permanent, and I have heard how he used to 'work at his scores' by sitting in an armchair with his eyes shut for some time. There might be an occasional interruption, when he would sit up with a growl, seize some music paper, and write on it in absolutely accurate full score three or four bars of a Beethoven symphony, or whatever it was, and then sit back and shut his eyes again. I can only suppose that the bars in question had not come to him instantly from their cold storage, and the act of writing them out would make them come to call immediately.

Another instance of his extreme power of, so to speak, visualizing the sound of music from the sight of the printed page was told me by an American colleague of his, who at a rehearsal heard him stop at a certain chord when he was rehearsing a brand new work by a young Italian composer for its first performance. Toscanini stopped, and said: 'Where is the oboe?' The point was that the oboe should have had a note contributing to the chord, which was already doubled in another part of the orchestra. Toscanini missed the oboe tone from the sound of that chord, even though the particular note concerned was being contributed by someone else as well. Toscanini's visual preparation of the score was so intense that the sound was also complete in his mind.

His actual stick technique was poor compared with Nikisch's. It didn't matter, because he had everything else. But with Nikisch everything was shown by the actual movement of the point of the stick. I was most interested to see in Malko's book on conducting his confirmation of my memory—that two fingers and the thumb sufficed for Nikisch to control his stick in this wonderfully expressive way. With Toscanini I think three or four fingers as well as the thumb were involved, and it was mostly through a movement of the arm that the stick moved.

The point of the stick said nothing special; it was simply that it swung along in an irresistible way naturally, with that tremendous mind and concentration behind it. But it did not swing along in an expressive way or a way that in itself could have contributed a great deal to the performance.

I have been asked whether his beat was perhaps clearer and the point of his stick more expressive at rehearsal than at performance. I don't think there was much difference between the two. Toscanini's movement came largely from his elbow and forearm and the expression in it came from behind the stick: it was in his mind all the time. His left hand was expressive, not used a great deal, but when it was there it was far more expressive than the right, because it was a natural limb while the stick that Toscanini used was a pretty heavy one.

WEINGARTNER

An early impression of Weingartner will never be dimmed: the seventh Symphony and *Egmont* overture in St James's Hall in November 1902. To a thirteen-year-old this new mercurial light on Beethoven, in a hall which was considerably smaller and more intimate than Queen's Hall, was almost overpowering and, coupled with Weingartner's very economical gestures and dominating command of structure, made a permanent impression.

A man of wide interests, composer and writer, he always gave the impression of an intellectual and seemed in command of anything he touched. Early in his life he gained a special reputation for his Beethoven performances, and this perhaps caused him to write a great deal about the performance of Beethoven and even to publish a book describing, bar by bar, his suggestions for alterations in scoring and dynamics. At one point in the development of the *Eroica* he mentions how, at a sequential passage, at the third repetition of which Beethoven adds trumpets and drums (because the chord contained a note they could contribute) he had decided to fill out each stage of the sequence in the same way, using the modern chromatic refinements. He was called one day (about the time of writing the book) to conduct the work at short notice when his own orchestral material was unavailable, and found that the entrance of drums and trumpets at the third repetition of the sequence was unexpectedly exciting, and so he suggests that orchestras should not necessarily adopt his additions at this point, for he felt that probably Beethoven knew best after all. On the occasion of his last visit to England a friend of mine asked him some question about the book. 'You have that book of mine on re-scoring Beethoven?' asked the great man. 'Then please will you go home and take it from your shelf and put it into your waste-paper basket?' In his maturity he had come to the conclusion that Beethoven didn't need all this doctoring. Another example of his honesty and humility was seen when he wrote repudiating his former poor opinion of Brahms, and said that it was only in middle age that he had come to recognize him at his full stature.

Weingartner was one of the earliest of the great internationals to visit us and play with the B.B.C. Orchestra after its formation in 1930, and his enthusiasm for the young organization was most refreshing to hear, and helped us a good deal with people who were wondering whether the B.B.C. Orchestra really was as good as we thought. He was by no means a narrow specialist, and in particular had a great respect for Berlioz. He was one of the editors of the new critical edition of Berlioz, which was in preparation just before the 1914 war, and he gave an electric performance of the Fantastic Symphony for us in 1933.

His manner on the platform was most reserved and

economical and his wrist did most of the work of propelling the stick. I once heard the wife of a rival conductor saying with contempt: 'Weingartner boasts that he can always go out to a party after a concert without even changing his collar.' We know that conductors vary a good deal in this respect, but it isn't always the hottest people who steer the ship with the greatest authority.

FURTWÄNGLER

Furtwängler was a dedicated and intensely emotional conductor. His stick, in comparison with Nikisch's, was inexpressive and difficult to follow. Furtwängler's behaviour at a concert was something that often made players extremely frightened because they felt that the body and soul of the music might not keep together. His beat, particularly to orchestras that didn't know him well, was extremely puzzling, and there were very often several beats at once—a sort of shaky, vibrant repetition of the beat, which made the audience wonder which of the repetitions was going to be chosen by the orchestra for the impact of the sound. It always seemed a miracle that they did in fact come in together. Furtwängler's concentration had chosen for them.

Now this, extended over a concert, had a very sharp effect on at least one distinguished player in the orchestra, who said that he was worn out at the end of the concert with the effort of finding out where he was and playing his part in the *ensemble*, and in an *ensemble* that really was an *ensemble*. And I am inclined to think that it was this tension, this uncertainty, that contributed a great deal to the magnetic power and warmth of the tone quality that came from Furtwängler's performances. If an orchestra doesn't quite know where it is, it plays with a certain intensity that contributes enormously to the vitality of the performance. The players as they play are really not sure whether they will put a foot wrong at any moment in any bar, and so they play with a certain excited vitality that contributes something remarkable to the power of the performance as a whole.

With a conductor who has a clear enough beat the orchestra know where they are, but they may not be on their toes to that extent and perhaps may not give so vital a performance. That is always a possibility.

It is of course conceivable that conductors who have a good deal of rehearsal time get a great deal of perfection, and use a technique which is so precise and easy to follow that the players sink back and need some other stimulus to make the performance vital. I cannot think of any extreme case, but it could be a great danger that a man who is in complete command of his technique, which might even be reasonably expressive, still gets as a result dull performances when he is not on top of his form, and particularly perhaps when he is thinking too much on architectural lines.

I feel sure, however, that it is extremely useful for a conductor in this country, who has very little rehearsal time, to have that extreme clarity. He can get over to the orchestra very quickly what he wants and make it clear to them, and there is no time for the performance to get stale.

BEECHAM

Absolute power over the orchestra was of course evident in the work of Sir Thomas Beecham. He had a most expressive stick, movements that were sometimes out of proportion when one compared them with the extreme economy of people like Nikisch and Bruno Walter; but there was a whole-hearted concentration and a wonderful power of expression. In fact very often he was able to persuade us that music that we had hitherto thought was not quite in the front rank was all the same something particularly lovely. It appealed so to him that he infectiously made it appeal to us.

It was almost a hypnotic appeal that he had over the orchestra, and with him it was perhaps even more a case of improvisation than it was with Furtwängler or Nikisch. It was quite well known and recognized in the orchestral world that what Beecham did in rehearsal he was not necessarily going to do at the performance. He might whip up something quite different and in quite a different manner. But it didn't matter. It was a lovely and lively experience that could be enjoyed by the whole audience as a *tour de force* and as a brilliant piece of musical exposition.

WOOD

With Sir Henry Wood there was again a perfection of stick technique. It was not as expressive as Nikisch's, but it was absolutely clear and understandable, and I think it was allied to the finest craftsmanship that any conductor in all time has exercised.

The amount of time he spent in preparation of his scores and parts was quite incredible and, as one has seen in Mr Bernard Shore's *The Orchestra Speaks*, much of the orchestral material in Sir Henry Wood's library had actually been marked at the top 'Corrected by Henry J. Wood', and every detail, bowing, phrasing, and, still more, the exact way in which the passage was going to be conducted, was shown clearly on those parts.

Early in his career he had the prodigious job of conducting six Promenade Concerts on three rehearsals each week for eight or ten weeks. He went on doing that for a number of years, and of course in order to do that without disaster one had got to think ahead to every detail and even to every *rallentando*, to decide just where one was going to break from the crotchet beat into quavers, so that the *rallentando* might be held together. This was all marked in his parts and in the score so that there was never any question of his doing anything different at any time.

And that is the fundamental difference between him and Thomas Beecham, who would improvise at a performance, and bring off that performance; with Wood it was all carefully and accurately prepared.

His rehearsal technique was as completely successful and well thought out as everything else concerned with his art. He planned his rehearsals to the minute, in fact to the half-minute. And soloists and concertos and everything, all fell into that scheme exactly. He would often play straight through a work at rehearsal, since he had a strong feeling that mistakes might occur in anything that had not been played, actually played, on the morning of a performance. And so he would do what in the opinion of many might incline the orchestra to dullness: playing straight through a work, not seriously minding how carefully or carelessly it was being played. However, it always took life at the performance.

He might shout a comment, that such and such a passage should be louder or softer, but he wouldn't necessarily stop and do it again.

During the Promenade season, when he was working very hard, he would save his arm a certain amount by letting his leader conduct. In this case he would go into the circle of Queen's Hall and sit with a little dinner bell, which he would ring if he wanted to stop and comment on anything. Sometimes this dinner bell disappeared mysteriously, but another one always appeared the next day. I think there was a store of them concealed somewhere.

Wood excelled in giving a clear performance of a work and putting it over so faithfully that one could go away and think it out for oneself afterwards and not have another mind in between one and the work, as one might have with Furtwängler or Beecham.

There is no doubt that his ideal was always to produce a faithful reproduction of the composer's will, with no varnishing and no embellishments from the performer. He was the kind of performer who prefers to feel that he is the servant of the composer without adding something personal to the composition.

And that was why composers of his day were delighted when he would give a first performance of a work, because they knew that it would come over absolutely crystal clear, and if anybody afterwards would like to start an individual interpretation of it, well, that would be all right, but first of all Wood put the thing before the public clearly as the composer had written it.

For six years, while I was at school, I was the proud possessor of a season ticket for all his winter concerts. In this way I came to know the whole of the classical repertoire and much else, in his sound, healthy, and dynamic performances. It was a wonderful initiation for a young musician.

STRAUSS

Richard Strauss was another conductor who, though he might be expected when conducting the works of other composers to interpose his own very strong personality, did not do so. He was a model of economy. In fact I would put him and Weingartner almost beside Nikisch.

Like Henry Wood, he was very professional. He was an easy rehearser, but a very intense rehearser of things that mattered to him, and I remember that the rather ominous summer of 1914 was lit up by a wonderful performance that he gave of his three early tone poems, followed by the Mozart G minor Symphony. It was said that being given six hours' rehearsal, he disposed of his own work in less than an hour and spent the remaining five working on the G minor. It certainly was a wonderful performance and obviously the result of much thought and preparation and precision of rehearsal. The surprisingly slow *tempo* of the first and last movements struck us at the time, also the fact that it did not *seem* at all slow, because his accentuation was so widely spaced that the music appeared to flow along quite swiftly.

A thoughtful friend of mine has linked Strauss's precise rehearsal craftsmanship with his love of card games; his care in planning his resources in rehearsal was in parallel with his playing of a hand of his favourite skat.

WALTER

Bruno Walter was one of the greatest conductors in the twenty or thirty years after Nikisch. He had of course a wonderful training with Mahler in

Vienna, and when in 1912 he took over in Munich he was ready to give the most superb performances of operas in many differing fields.

I was lucky enough to hear his first performance in Munich in 1912 of the three great Mozart operas. Then, during the war, he did a very great deal to encourage and display the work of German composers. People like Braunfels and Pfitzner owed everything to Bruno Walter at that time. And when one was able to get back to Munich in the twenties, Walter was in command of a wonderful *ensemble*, in command of every school of opera, with the option of using three different houses, each ideally suited to the style of opera that was being performed.

His stick technique was simple and economical, and he gave himself completely to any work that he took over. I have seen him white as a sheet after a symphonic performance; a work like the Schubert C major would tax him to the utmost. But that was the nature of his concentration and the nature of his outlook on music. And music as a mission, something that could inspire and make finer people, not only of those taking part, but of those listening in the audience, was the ideal of this great man.

That sense of dedication was a great force, almost a moral force with him. It is rare among performers, perhaps, but I have met it not only in Walter. There are others who belong to the type of artist who never seems to place himself between the music and the people to whom he is playing or before whom he is conducting. Yehudi Menuhin is one. I feel with him as I felt with Walter, Toscanini, and, indeed, Casals, that the music always came first and was of first consequence all the time.

Walter's contact with the orchestra was as magnetic as

that of any conductor I have mentioned. It was got by rather different means from those used by Toscanini and Furtwängler. It was the man's complete sincerity that came from him to the players and so to the audience; that and his great humility. His idea was that every member of his orchestra was a human being who thought and breathed and loved his music just as he did himself, and was always to be encouraged to do so more and more.

In his rehearsals he stopped a fair amount. He had very clear ideas about what he wanted and he perhaps went into detail more than most conductors. He could make active use of a long period of rehearsal in such a way that the orchestra was fascinated and wanted to go further. I expect many readers will have heard the two delightful records that have been published of a rehearsal with Bruno Walter of a Mozart symphony, and I can cordially recommend them as a tonic; they show how a great man can dedicate himself to the spiritual importance of music, even while he is dealing with technical points.

CONDUCTOR-SOLOISTS AND SOLOIST-CONDUCTORS

It is worth remembering that Bruno Walter sometimes liked to play and conduct a concerto at the same time. In the small Mozarteum at Salzburg, with a group of the Vienna Philharmonic sitting round him, there were enchanting performances of Mozart piano concertos.

In my B.B.C. days we tried to transport these performances to Queen's Hall. There it seemed necessary to have a bigger orchestra, and the intimacy disappeared altogether. To anyone who had heard the Salzburg performances, the Queen's Hall performance was a

Richard Strauss with the author during the interval of a broadcast concert, 1947.

Bruno Walter, at the age of seventy-eight, at rehearsal with the B.B.C. Symphony Orchestra, 1955.

Felix Weingartner.

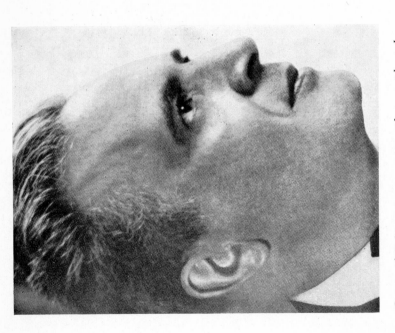

Bruno Walter; a portrait photograph taken

disappointment. And I think that brings us back to a tradition of music-making, that if a piano plays with strings, more than a quintet is not usually very satisfactory. It is true Walter had a good many more than a quintet at Salzburg, but there is a limit to the number that you can have.

In America, where this method of concerto playing and conducting had become a feature about ten years ago, I heard Iturbi playing the Grieg Concerto with the Philadelphia Orchestra; it ought to have been all right, but it most emphatically wasn't. The famous scales in the last movement finishing with a crack of the full orchestra, I admit, are rather a terror to the conductor—I'm never quite happy about them myself. But on this occasion Iturbi got comfortably to the A at the top of the scale and the orchestra came in comfortably on its crash an appreciable split second after he had finished his scale.

I know that Mitropoulos has sometimes played even Prokofief concertos with the New York orchestra, but I doubt whether this can ever be satisfactory. Control from the keyboard is just not practical politics with an orchestra larger than twenty or twenty-five. It may have been all very well in Bach's day, though there are many of us who are not quite sure that the performances that Bach heard of his own works were of the standard that we expect nowadays.

Certain artists who are great teachers have also been conductors of considerable character.

First of all in this connection I think of Pau Casals. I had the great experience of spending a month in Barcelona in the days when he was conducting an orchestra which he had collected there, and which was costing him much time and money. It was a delightfully easy-going

Spanish kind of procedure. I remember the rehearsals finished each morning at 12.30 a.m. He rehearsed very thoroughly, as if it were chamber music, and I had the pleasure of listening to the detailed rehearsals of many varied things. Casals's range of interest was surprising, spreading naturally over the great Viennese period, but including Stravinsky, Saint-Saëns, and many other composers of all schools. When he came to London after the formation of the B.B.C. Symphony Orchestra, we often asked him to conduct an afternoon concert on the Sunday and play a concerto at one of the Wednesday evening Queen's Hall concerts. We always learnt a great deal and in particular I can remember very fine performances of the Brahms *Tragic* Overture and the Schubert C major Symphony conducted by him.

I think it was with him a pretty stern rule that he would never play the cello on occasions when he was conducting. He certainly never conducted a cello concerto which he was himself playing, and always kept the two functions entirely separate. His rehearsal technique seemed more like a lesson from a great teacher than anything else; he did not trouble very much to make his stick an expressive instrument.

But when he was rehearsing, he would actually teach the players how to play their instruments; bowing and phrasing as well as interpretation. Much as he was interested in the technique of stringed instruments, he would use similar methods with wind players.

In more recent times Mr Menuhin has taken to conducting string organizations. He usually leads as well, and I always think that when a small string combination plays with a leader of that calibre, provided the bass is also led by a musician of some sensitiveness and understanding, a performance of a peculiar lilt and beauty can emerge, such as can very often elude even the most sensitive stick.

COMPOSER-CONDUCTORS

I suppose we use composers as conductors more in this country than in other countries. Elgar of course conducted his own works with great authority. I have often been asked if he was a good conductor. He was and he wasn't. Nobody I have ever met will admit that they have ever heard a finer performance of an Elgar work than those conducted by Elgar himself. And there is no question about it—he had a particular sense of that nervous power that did make his music. Now it doesn't always apply that a composer is a really fine conductor of his own music. Many of them are efficient conductors and get quite good results, except that they get too excited to start with and the whole thing lacks balance and structure and a sense of climax. Strauss of course was such an experienced conductor that he could do it all right. But then Strauss did conduct other people's music as well as his own; Elgar did so only for a short period in middle life, when he was engaged to conduct a tour and a whole season by the London Symphony Orchestra. It was not a great success: it didn't last very long. It was chiefly as a conductor of his own music that he is remembered.

One weakness shown by most composer-conductors comes from their inability to hear what is happening because they hear what they want to hear, and fail to get a balanced performance because their ears are so full of what should be there. If it isn't there they don't notice it. They have got their vision of the work as they originally heard it and wrote it down and they can't find out how what they are actually hearing differs from their vision and put into words the difference, so that the players concerned, and singers, can adapt themselves to it. They cannot get outside their own music.

Vaughan Williams always gave a most memorable performance of the *London Symphony*—it is sad that this was never recorded. Many passages where most of us are tempted to linger a bit, and make the most of the expressiveness, were simply played through by him: he didn't want any nonsense about it: it could carry its own message without embellishment. He rushed through it and somehow it sounded absolutely splendid. I'm afraid I should never dare to copy his reading.

There was a good story about a particularly fine performance which he conducted in Buffalo, U.S.A. He always marked his own scores a good deal to help him to conduct, in very large blue pencil. And particularly where there were bars moving fast—one in a bar or two in a bar —he numbered the bars so that he could feel his way along as he went. The score which he had marked for this Buffalo performance suddenly disappeared just before the performance took place, and he had to use another virgin copy, which made him very angry, with the result that the performance gained magnificently in intensity. He was rather amused to tell the story afterwards, because the full score was discovered very close to him. It had been shut up inside the grand piano.

When Vaughan Williams took over the London Bach Choir, he asked the committee to allow him to have no concert at all for the whole of the first winter, but to devote it to the study of Bach's *St Matthew Passion*. At the end, when Easter time came, he gave about half a dozen performances of it, in various places, with different sections of the choir. It was a most moving and interesting performance. I heard the first of them. He took some arbitrary liberties with Bach which are not perhaps to everyone's taste, and these he developed more and more at the annual performance, which made a deep impression in connection with the Dorking Festivals, and was repeated with the Hallé Orchestra and Choir in Manchester, within a year or two of his death. The paramount impression on me, when I first heard the London *St Matthew Passion*, before Vaughan Williams had done it many times, was that it was not a fine piece of conducting, as such, at all. It was that a very great musician indeed had worked for six months with a large number of intelligent people, and at the end of it he had impressed the whole society with his own view of the Bach *St Matthew Passion* so that the production of it was not conducting in the customary sense. The performance could not proceed except as it had been rehearsed and rehearsed: Bach through the spectacles of Ralph Vaughan Williams. It was a spiritual matter.

Postlude

THIS book is full of detailed ideas mainly concerned with some aspects of the technique of the art. That is natural, but we must not forget that the fundamentals of all music-making apply to a conductor as much as to anyone else—indeed more, because the conductor's task must include the teaching of others, and whether he wishes it or not, this is bound to carry with it a profound influence over all those with whom he comes in contact. For this reason it is greatly to be deplored when conductors make use of their position to exploit their power, and try to make bosses of themselves, when their position should surely be more like that of the chairman of a committee. The conductor at rehearsal naturally has to instruct and command, but he must be quite certain that he is not trying to command people who know more about the detail of the matter in hand than he does himself. Even if he knows more than anyone round him, he is still the servant of the composer, and I have had the privilege of hearing Toscanini talking about Beethoven, and Bruno Walter discussing Mozart, both with the profoundest admiration, reverence and humility. The greatest interpreters (not only conductors) venerate the composers they serve and yield to none in their simple delight in the new beauties that continually emerge from the greatest works of art as long as one has any sensitive contact with them.

POSTLUDE

I have said that conducting is the youngest form of artistic expression, and has not yet crystallized into 'schools'. This is obvious to anyone who visits the Royal Festival Hall at all often, and much that is in this book is controverted on that platform almost every night. Great performances are heard there all the same, and I am often impressed by the power that can be exercised by a conductor whose technique is rudimentary, but who has real integrity, musicianship and concentration, coupled with a sense of dedicated service to the composer whose work he is performing.

The qualities we have just mentioned, when the conductor can command them, and can add a determination that each performance he ever gives shall be more eloquent than the one before, will help him on the way to a missionary dissemination of fine music finely performed. Just as Beethoven in later life reached a sublimity undreamed of in middle age, so can his servant the interpreter fix his ambition on a range of expression that will steadily deepen and purify, not only his own experience, but that of his colleagues on the platform and his friends in the audience; and will help him to pass his message far beyond the walls of the hall where he is working, and so enable the noble spirituality of great music to spread far and wide, even including its healing power, which is only now beginning to be understood.

BIBLIOGRAPHY

Boult, Adrian C., 1920, *The Technique of Conducting*, Hall the Printer, Oxford.

Bowles, Michael, 1961, *The Conductor: His Artistry and Craftsmanship*, G. Bell.

Braithwaite, Warwick, 1952, *The Conductor's Art*, Williams & Norgate.

Brook, Donald, 1946, *Conductors' Gallery*, Rockliff Publishing Corporation.

——, 1951, *New International Gallery of Conductors*, Rockliff Publishing Corporation.

Ewen, David, 1936, *The Man with the Baton*, New York.

Geissmar, B., 1944, *The Baton and the Jackboot*, Hamish Hamilton.

Goldbeck, F., 1960, *The Perfect Conductor*, Dobson.

Holmes, Malcolm H., 1951, *Conducting an Amateur Orchestra*, Oxford University Press and Harvard University Press.

Inghelbrecht, D. E., 1953, *The Conductor's World*, Peter Neville.

Malko, N., 1950, *The Conductor and his Baton*, Novello.

Munch, Charles, 1955, *I am a Conductor*, Oxford University Press and New York.

Scherchen, H., 1933, *Handbook of Conducting*, Oxford University Press.

Shore, B., 1938, *The Orchestra Speaks*, Longmans.

BIBLIOGRAPHY

Wagner, Richard, 1940 (4th ed.), *On Conducting*, trans. E. Dannreuther, W. Reeves.

Walter, Bruno, 1961, *Of Music and Music-Making*, trans. P. Hamburger, Faber.

Weingartner, Felix, 1906, *On Conducting*, trans. Ernest Newman, Breitkopf and Haertel, Leipzig.

——, *Ratschläge für Aufführungen klassischer Symphonien*:
Vol. I, 1916, *Beethoven*, Leipzig.
Vol. II, 1918, *Schubert & Schumann*, Leipzig.
Vol. III, 1923, *Mozart*, Leipzig.

Wood, Sir Henry J., 1945, *About Conducting*, Sylvan Press.

Woodgate, Leslie (Foreword by Adrian C. Boult), 1944, *The Chorus Master*, Ascherberg.

——, 1949, *The Choral Conductor*, Ascherberg.

Wright, Denis, 1948, *The Brass Band Conductor*, Joshua Duckworth, Colne.

Index

INDEX

INDEX

Intonation, 26
Iturbi, José, 65

KLEIBER, ERICH, 46
Klemperer, Otto, 25
Knowledge, of score, 8, 11, 13, 38, 42

LEADER, Orchestra, 27
Left hand, 3, 6, 55
Legge, Walter, 3
Lewis, Joseph, 5
Liszt, xii
London Symphony Orchestra, 67
Long notes, followed by short, 21–2
Looking-glass, use of, 3

MAHLER, Gustav, 18, 41, 62
Malko, 54
Marking scores, 12
Maryon, Edward, absolute pitch, 12
Memory, conducting from, 14
Mengelberg, Willem, 9
Mensendieck, xv
Menuhin, Yehudi, 63, 66
Metronome, watch used as, 11
Miniature scores, 13
Minuet and trio, uniform speed, 10
Mitropoulos, Dmitri, 65
Mozart, Wolfgang Amadeus, 24
  Figaro in Munich, 41

G minor Symphony, 10
Pianoforte concertos, 32, 64–65
repeats, 46
Strauss, 62
style, 9
Walter, 41, 63, 64, 71
Munich, 63

NATIONAL temperaments, 16–17
Nerves, 43–4
Nikisch, Arthur, ix–x, xii, 48–52
  applause, x
  and Beecham, 59
  Beethoven, x
  Brahms, x
  Butterworth, 49–50
  choral method, 30–1
  economy, x, 2
  eloquence, 3
  fingers, wrist, elbow, 3–4
  grip, of stick, 54
  left hand, 3, 49
  opera, 41
  rehearsals, 15, 17, 19, 20, 27, 48–9
  and Richter, x
  and Strauss, 62
  Tchaikovsky, xii
  Wagner, x, xii, 41, 50
  and Wood, 59
Nyemann, Mrs Harriet, xv

OPERA, 40–2
Oxford, 31

INDEX

PACE, *see* Speed
Palestrina, 9
Parts, marks in, 12
Performance, 43–7
  clear, 61
  ultimate aim of, 7
  starting, 6
  vitality, 58
Pfitzner, Hans, 63
Philadelphia, 14, 65
Pianoforte, concertos, 36
  position of conductor, 36
  stick of, 36
Platform plan, 22
Point of stick, 3, 4, 5, 6
  Beecham, 19
  expression, 5
  Nikisch, 48–9
  opera, 41
  Toscanini, 54–5
Porteous baton, 4–5
Preparation of scores, 7–8
  for performance, 43–4
  Sir Henry Wood, 59–60
Prokofief, Serge, 65
Promenade Concerts, 60

QUEEN'S HALL, 16, 34, 64, 66

RACHMANINOFF, 36
Recitatives, 38
Reger, Max, 50
Rehearsals, 15–31
  atmosphere, 19, 71
  for choir, 29

  conductor's comments, 19
  Nikisch, 49
  speed of, 27
  split, 26
  Strauss, 62
  like teaching, 21
  tension, 16
  time-table, 18
  Toscanini, 52
  Wood, 60
Repeats, 46
Richter, Hans, as horn player, xi
  Meistersinger, x, xi
  and Nikisch, x
  popularity, xi
  second violins, 24
  separated basses, 23
  Siegfried Idyll, xii
  standing still, 2
Rimsky-Korsakov, 23
Rite of Spring, 16
Rostrum, height of, 24–5
Royal Ballet, 42
Royal Festival Hall, 22, 23, 72

SAFONOFF, WASSILY, xii
St James's Hall, 55
Salzburg, 64–5
Sargent, (Sir) Malcolm, 36
Schools of conducting, ix, 72
Schubert, C major Symphony,
  Casals, 66
  speed, 9
  style, 20
  Walter, 63

INDEX